RED STATE CONFESSIONS

TIM TUCKER

How does a confirmed liberal Democrat evolve into a straight-ticke
Trump-voting, conservative Republican? Here is the story of on
voter's journey from left to right, how he got there and what issue
matter most in today's convoluted political battlefield. Included ar
essays on Trump, immigration, abortion, the economy, the new
media, race, gun violence, prejudice against the South, and prediction
for the 2020 elections. A good read that will challenge your beliefs an
may surprise you before you finish this timely story.

Tim Tucker
High Point, NC
www.redstateconfessions.com

To Karen, Heather, and my late father,

who often told me...

"There are three sides to every issue...

yours, mine and the facts"

Introduction

In 2008, our nation held a national presidential election. My preferred candidate lost. Another election was conducted four years later and once again, my candidate came in second. Both times, I did what I thought was the American thing to do...I went home, licked my wounds, and prayed that the new president would guide the country through troubled waters without too much partisan politics and that the nation would survive and thrive even if his beliefs and policies were vastly different than my own.

Actually, my reaction to the results in these contests was less remarkable by what I did than by what I *didn't* do. I didn't travel to the inauguration to scream profanities through bullhorns or set overturned cars ablaze. I didn't attend rallies in the nation's capital to protest the election of a man who had yet to give a speech, pass a law, or nominate a Supreme Court judge. I did not plaster my car with stickers that read *"Not My President,"* nor did I don a *"Resistance"* ball cap. I didn't register at a website advocating the assassination of the president or photograph myself holding a bloody head of the sitting president.

That is just a partial sampling of the insanity I have beheld since November of 2016, when the candidate of my choice did prevail against the most powerful political machine this country has ever known (the Clintons) and won the nomination in the manner by which we select presidents in this democracy. I thought that I had observed every form of unrest and disappointment in my forty plus years of political participation, but the circus I have watched since this election makes the 1968 Chicago riots look like a bad night at roller derby.

I have watched in disbelief as actors stopped a performance on Broadway to insult the vice president of the United States and his wife during a play. I have read stories of restaurateurs and wait staff refusing to serve cabinet members and their families for dinner. I have heard major Hollywood stars wishing that the White House would burn down and another who suggested that the president's son be put in a cage with a convicted child molester. And worst of all, to my way of thinking, I have watched as the first lady has been brutalized by the press in a manner I never thought I would see in my lifetime.

Meanwhile, the candidate I voted for has persevered, ignoring these onslaughts, energizing our economy, putting millions of people to work, reducing the welfare roles, stimulating the business sector, and working diligently to protect our borders by enforcing immigration laws that have been on the books for decades.

For me, the collective opposition to this president has taken a personal toll. For the first time in my life, I have been deemed a racist, homophobe, misogynist (whatever that is), and a white supremacist, a classification that is so bizarre I find it difficult to comprehend. People I have known for decades have shunned me, and friendships have een broken, even though I work hard to keep my personal politics to myself.

ince personal conversations and attempts to express my positions in logical and rational manner have disintegrated into contentious ersonal quarrels, I have decided to express my thoughts in this book, where I cannot be interrupted or shouted down before I finish a ohesive sentence. I consider it my personal statement on this madness, and I hope that somebody somewhere will be reminded that eople can disagree without hating one another.

also hope that I can remind voters about the issues that are really mportant to everyday Americans, the life we live, and the future we ollectively face. I want folks to realize the radicals marching in the treets, accusing the president of unending crimes without evidence re simply attempting to create a smokescreen that obscures their ctual agenda, a plan that will undo every accomplishment of the last our years simply to achieve their only true goal, to remove the sitting resident and regain political power.

realize that one such effort by this insignificant private citizen will e met with the same personal attacks on me, my family, and my eliefs, but I have warned them, and they have collectively sent me a message....

Ve think the country is worth it.

CONFESSION

I Was Once A Liberal

I was raised in a straight-laced, highly religious, conservative home. We went to church every time the doors were open, prayed before meals, recited the Pledge of Allegiance with conviction, put our hands over our hearts and saluted the flag. I attended John Glenn High School in his home town, a school that required History, Latin and U.S. Government in a class taught by a hard line constitutionalist who expected you to know how our government works, how it has evolved since the founding fathers, and to learn every line of the constitution and the amendments to the same.

I graduated in 1968, when John Glenn himself placed a diploma in my hand. Then off to college I went, with the money my father provided me, in the car my he bought me, and an education compliments of his ifetime dedication to hard, backbreaking work. Upon arriving on campus, I looked out at the sea of long-haired, sandal wearing young adults and decided that my youth had been wasted on boring, bible-thumping, overly-patriotic endeavors that were forced on me by an adult world that just didn't understand the world as it really was (and, of course, I did.)

I promptly ditched my crew cut for long shaggy locks, donned bell bottom jeans, sandals and a dirty t-shirt. I then traded my nice new car for a Volkswagen which I plastered with bumper stickers that read *"No Nukes!"* and *"Impeach Nixon"* along with various other messages I felt were critical for me to broadcast. I viewed myself as a non-conformist who had joined forces with those that would save the world from Armageddon. When I returned home for a visit, I explained to my father that his life in the discovery of natural gas had been wasteful and destructive, lectured him on the impending destruction of the planet, then asked him for more money before heading back to the campus in time for a protest march. I don't remember what the protest was about, just that it was terribly important and more fun than attending class.

Before I knew it, I was no longer a college student. I was an unemployed hippie with a beautiful young wife and child, no job, no degree and bills to pay. Soon, reality began to sink in. Protest marches didn't pay well (then) and long-haired, bell-bottomed hippies were not in great demand. I cut my hair, washed my face, bought some regular clothes and went looking for a job. I fancied myself a writer and soon landed a job writing obituaries for the Southeast Missourian, a century old newspaper whose offices overlooked the Mississippi River. My weekly paycheck was $100.00 with take-home pay of $84.61, out of which I paid for a car, apartment, and groceries. It was a sobering but exhilarating experience. I was now a husband, father and taxpayer. I didn't have time to march or protest...I had mouths to feed.

The next few years passed quickly. Eventually I was able to start a small business doing screen printing on t-shirts, signs and bumper stickers. Now, I had employees, commercial rent, margins to meet, suppliers to pay and a bank loan to honor. At the time, I was borrowing money at one over prime, which was in the high teens. Since I slept through most of my college business classes, I did not realize that one cannot run a wholesale business, pay employees and Federal taxes, then borrow money at 18% and expect to make a profit.

About this time, I began to experience a series of personal epiphanies, in which I reviewed my adult life up to that point, the idiotic decisions I had made and the ridiculous assumptions I had drawn with no logical support whatsoever. It hit me that I knew very little about Richard Nixon and even less about nuclear power, except that it was, well, nuclear. I suddenly saw that my college age transformation did not make me a nonconformist. Instead, it made me the ultimate conformist. In my world of that time, everyone had long hair and sandals, drove Volkswagens and marched in the street. I wasn't a rebel...I was an ignorant donkey following a carrot hung from a stick in front of my naive and youthful face.

Now I was a father, husband, parent, business owner, taxpayer and voter...a voter who had hoisted himself up by his own petard by helping a wonderful, sincere man named Jimmy Carter. I loved the man...he was determined, optimistic, compassionate and a confirmed liberal Democrat. Now I had the privilege to see a true liberal in action. I watched cluelessly as he raised the prime rate to nearly 20%, tried to cure inflation with price freezes (which never work), raised gas prices and put the country on an *"every other day"* gas ration, then, just to put a cherry on top of an administrative disaster, boycotted the 1980 Olympics, ruining the professional careers of athletes who had spent their entire young lives training for an opportunity that would be snatched from them by a liberal ideologue to protest a war in Afghanistan, an act that almost ruined an international sporting contest that had survived war and conflict for decades, since his action caused the Russians to boycott the next Olympics, compromising the integrity of the Olympics for more than 20 years. The day he left office, fifty-two Americans citizens were being held hostage as they had been for 444 days. That was January 20, 1981, the day that a conservative leader named Ronald Reagan took over. Magically, the hostages came home.

Jimmy Carter's policies embody everything that is wrong (and dangerous) about liberalism. It sounds good, feels good, but it doesn't work...and in a capitalistic democracy, things have to WORK. People have to work, government has to work, businesses have to work and corporate America has to work. It is not pretty or fun but that is the way it is in the real world.

In the late sixties and early seventies, thousands of idealistic minded young hippies decided to establish their own socialistic versions of paradise, which they optimistically labeled *"communes."* Everyone chipped in, planted the crops and picked the fruits of their labors, and everyone was happy...for a while. Then some of them got lazy, others ambitious. Gradually, one after the other, these experiments failed as they are all destined to do. Now, most of those communal socialists are trading stocks, running giant software firms, or panhandling on the streets of San Francisco.

For me, my view of the world was changing as my life changed. Raising a child and running a business will do that. It teaches you discipline and competition, that the world as you wish it was and the world as it is are two completely different realities; one that is full of incense and peppermint, another that is full of harsh realities and tough decisions. The idea that my national government would provide my every need once held the same attraction as those hippie communes, but I slowly came to the realization that every carrot comes with a stick, primarily in the form of higher taxes and government interference into my personal affairs and decisions.

It is no wonder to me that today's youngsters are drawn to socialism. Why not? Virtually all of them have been living in a socialist nirvana for the first 18 years of their life, with free rent, housing, meals and money, just as I did. For me, the end of the eternal hand-out was more personal. In the wee hours of January 1st, 1979 following a wild New Years Eve party, I received a phone call from my sister who informed

...e that my father, who was in perfect health and had always supported me through thick and thin, was dead of a heart attack. I was an extremely immature 29 years old.

I was on my own. This book describes my journey from then to now.

CONFESSION

I find liberalism to be irrational, illogical, and dangerous.

I have lived in North Carolina for forty years. I have watched as
evolved from a hard-working conservative state whose econom
revolved around tobacco, furniture, and textiles to a world-clas
economic powerhouse dependent upon technology, developmen
banking, and tourism. This new direction also brought us another nev
element...tons of liberal Democrats escaping the tax oppression of th
Northeast corridors. Plus, scores of college graduates arrived to sna
up the high-paying jobs to be found in business hubs like Raleigh'
Research Triangle Park, but the largest measurable populatio
demographic was baby boomers who were retiring from their jobs i
New York, New Jersey, and Connecticut to enjoy their sunset years in
place that actually has sunshine, not to mention bargain basement (b
their standards) real estate prices and minuscule tax bills. One woul

think they would view this economic and meteorological Shangri-la as a sign to reconsider their political views, but it didn't ...or hasn't to date. Thus this solid red state now has some blue pockets to be found in the Raleigh/Durham area, Charlotte, and Asheville, which by some quirk of fate now have nearly the highest real estate prices, highest overall tax burden (city and local, property, and sales taxes) but offer the lowest incidence of affordable single-family homes to be found anywhere in the state.

Not long ago, I found myself in downtown Raleigh (named after Sir Walter.) While waiting for my meeting in a swanky hotel, I stepped across the street to catch a bite in a popular national sandwich chain. I ordered, then picked up my sandwich of choice, and sat down at a bistro table. I found the sandwich a bit bland, so, although I seldom if ever add salt to my food, I felt this particular combo needed a sodium boost. I sauntered up to the counter and casually asked, "Could I have some salt?..Your condiment tray seems to be out," at which time, the cherubic-faced youngster behind the counter replied with a determined expression, "I'm sorry, sir. This restaurant does not offer salt in our restaurants." I stared at him in disbelief before returning to my chair.

For most people, this incident might have seemed only a minor inconvenience, but for me, it demonstrated just one more example of the abject insanity, and self-righteous condescension of the liberal philosophy and position. It isn't enough for them to decide what is good for them; they must force it on YOU. If they are vegetarians, they want to take away your meat.They can't just avoid fur; they must deface yours. If they dislike guns, they must disarm you. If they decide oil is the enemy, they must take away your car.

Liberals love to talk about "freedom," but no group in American history has had less understanding of it or a desire to offer it. Their concept of freedom is whatever THEY think is good, even if it is vulgar, ugly, unpatriotic, and morally reprehensible. They have spent the last forty years destroying every wholesome symbol of American culture and replacing it with a chaotic, dysfunctional message of anarchy and despair.   They have successfully removed religious symbols, public prayer, respect for law enforcement, support for the military, love of country, honoring our flag and anthem with a non-stop effort to destroy our country, our history, our culture, and the constitutional glue that holds this nation together. Apparently, they dislike this country and everything in it....all for reasons I have yet to fathom.

For me, the daily news is like a Monty Python show. I turn on the public channel and see someone extolling the virtues of "cage-free eggs." Like all liberal concepts, this seems so sensitive and caring...until you wake up on planet earth and look at the numbers. Americans purchase 229 MILLION DOZEN eggs per year. Imagine if all these laying chickens were running around on open farmland? It is a wonderful, bucolic image of Americana, but it would take half the country's real estate to meet the demand, and egg collection would be comical. Further, there is no evidence that this would produce a healthier, more earth-friendly egg. Contrast this with the liberal view that beef production occupies too much land, and you only begin to see the futility and absurdity of such positions.

Examples like this are so numerous, It would take an encyclopedia to compile them. From cow farts to "conflict diamonds," liberals are so removed from reality, it boggles the mind. While conservatives are trying to build businesses and keep people employed, the liberal illuminati is concentrated on removing gender specific pronouns (he, she, her, him), legalizing pot, assisted suicide and full-term abortion, and ensuring that transgender citizens have access to the public bathroom of their choice. Regardless of your position on these burning social issues, I can't help but wonder what would happen if these people are given control of our government again.

Liberalism persists because there are a substantial number of kind, considerate, and peace-loving people who see this position as the compassionate choice, over a party of rational and serious decision-makers who look at things as they are, not as we wish they were...then prioritize issues in terms of what is MOST IMPORTANT right now for the American people, not chickens.

Conservatism is not always pretty. Take Mrs. Johnson, who teaches fourth grade and finds out that one of her students needs a kidney transplant. Then, out of the blue, she decides to donate one of her kidneys to this child whom she barely knows. The liberal press lavishes praise on the unselfish act, and she is hailed a hero. However, as a conservative with an only child who has experienced health issues, I can't help but wonder what Mrs. Johnson will do when her own son or daughter comes to tell her that they need a kidney. What then? Does she tell them, "Sorry, I gave mine to a kid named Billy, who is now a surfer in Malibu?" No matter how selfish it may sound, you must take care of your own before you can rescue others. After all, you can't save a drowning man if you don't know how to swim.

However, liberals never let logic get in the way of a cool but dangerous idea, even if it takes us into outer space. In 1977, NASA launched the Voyager spacecraft into deep space to explore what lies beyond. It carried with it every possible piece of information about our planet. It included technical specifications about our globe, its size and composition, including resources like water and precious minerals. It included samples of every language on earth, mathematical formulas, photographs, recordings of music, and our technical knowledge about propulsion and space travel. On the front of the spacecraft, the message was engraved "We Come In Peace."

I'm sure the average liberal thinks this is the greatest outreach ever by mankind (sorry...humankind), but as a conservative, I honestly think it may be the single biggest mistake our species has ever made, and might very well spell our demise. As I see it, my logic goes like this. Either there is intelligent life out there or there isn't. If there is, the recipient of this information-packed message will be either behind us in technology, or far ahead of us. If they are far ahead of us, and in need of resources, then we are in big trouble.

or anyone who questions my logic, I suggest you look at every istorical meeting between two different species, from amoeba to inosaurs to humans. In each case, there has been conflict and onquest, with the loser reduced to slavery, food source, or nnihilation (ask America's Native Americans) or just look at the usiness plans of every new entrepreneurial rocket mission, like paceX. Every single plan includes a promise to investors that justifies ie mission and finances it with the potential mining of the estination planet and exploiting its resources. What about distant ravelers headed here? Do we think these cosmic visitors will build iterplanetary spacecraft and travel millions of miles just to say hello? ven some of the most liberal astronomers now recognize this danger.

have tons of liberal friends (or I did until the publication of this ook!), and they are all wonderful people. They drink foreign wine, uy foreign cars, listen to NPR, and refer to the United States as if it ere an embarrassing uncle who drinks too much at Thanksgiving. hey don't have a flag in the yard or a sticker on the car, and they tand for the pledge with a sneer. They think everything is better omewhere else...France...Canada...the Netherlands. It is difficult ometimes to understand why they are still here. It seems that they ersevere just to wait for a Democratic president, at which time they xpect everything to be okay again.

ou can forgive them for this optimism(?). After all, when a Democrat nters the White House, the country becomes a haven for peace and ranquility. Protesters disappear from the streets; foreign affairs seem to settle; police stop beating suspects; and the weather returns to just something we watch on the news. The hole in the ozone disappears and the oceans appear to settle into an acceptable level. Tornadoes and hurricanes become routine weather events, and Civil War statues become roosting spots for pigeons, just as they have for 125 years. Presidential press conferences become lovefests, and the streets of Washington, D.C., once again become the path of limos on the way to the next political fundraiser. No one attacks cabinet members at dinner or at Broadway plays. Even Republicans can relax and enjoy the fruits of their political spoils.

For me, the real danger is that there are two levels to the liberal Democratic Party. One is the loyal followers who sincerely believe that the issue at hand is the plight of immigrants, gays and lesbians, or the poor. The other level is the liberal illuminati who have an agenda that the average Democratic voter knows nothing about and few would support. As I see it, the liberal leadership has a long-term agenda in mind that includes items like the following..

1. Elimination of, or major revision to the Constitution

2. Elimination of the electoral college

3. Voting rights for illegal immigrants without citizenship

4. Expansion of the Supreme Court to fifteen

5. Elimination of states' rights

6. The United States to become part of a world union that eliminates national boundaries and sovereignty

7. Elimination of majority rule by U.S. voters

8. Control of health care and distribution of benefits

9. Drastic reduction of wealth by individual citizens and massive tax increases on those who pay taxes

10. Draconian legislation to eliminate or cripple the petroleum industry and use of fossil fuels for cars, planes, boats, or industry

That is just for a start. Number 7 may shock many of you, regardless of political loyalties. But the truth is, many things that have happened over the last twenty years would have shocked you at the time, but they happened nonetheless. It is called "creeping incrementalism," the slow but constant encroachment into social values that you accept without knowing it. What if I had predicted full-term abortion to you twenty years ago? Or the confiscation of personal weapons? The boundaries just keep moving unless you take a stand and draw a line in the sand. The elimination of majority rule may seem crazy now, but spend an hour with a true liberal away from the cameras and tape recorders. I promise you they will eventually tell you that the only reason that conservatives continue to win elections is that "the majority of voters are too ignorant to deserve the right to vote." Don't doubt me. They are not just coming for your guns, they are coming for your vote!

Evidence of the liberal desire to invoke minority rule is easy to find. In my home state of North Carolina, activists have spent the last three years destroying or removing statues that have been standing for more than one hundred years while authorities looked on. Meanwhile, the same groups prevailed upon the powers that be to rename our region's oldest fall festival because the name contained the word "Dixie." Like the statues, the Dixie Classic Fair had been celebrated without controversy for nearly one hundred and twenty years. In both cases, surveys of citizens in the affected regions revealed overwhelmingly that they opposed these changes, but change they did. For the record, I don't feel strongly about either issue, but I vehemently oppose mob rule or any removal of our historical icons without public mandate.

The most interesting element of liberal politics is that the majority of U.S. voters simply will not buy into these concepts unless they are camouflaged by temporary crises that blur the real issues that face voters at the time of election. At the time of this writing, the United States is experiencing the best economy in sixty years, with job growth in every demographic group, from women, Hispanics, and African Americans. Small businesses are flourishing, and "Help Wanted" signs are everywhere. But the current liberal Democratic Party has spent nearly four years doing nothing but trying to destroy the administration that delivered this boon to the nation, even if it means losing all these economic gains. Liberal pundits like Bill Maher openly pray for an economic recession, even if it means putting millions out of work. Obviously, these people care more about their agenda than the well-being of the American people.

Anyone who has doubts about the folly of liberal leadership of government need only take a close look at the state of California. This state is, and has always been, ruled by an extreme liberal Democratic cabal. The state has astronomical taxes, extreme environmental policies, endless laws and regulations. Yet, the problems they sought to rectify with this revenue are worse than anywhere else. Their beaches are fouled by pollution and are generally considered unsafe in most areas, while much of their cities are cloaked in smog. Meanwhile, the social issues that their political position claims as their top concern (and their taxes were supposed to cure) seem to be ignored and certainly unaddressed. Real estate prices and taxes make home ownership impossible for the poor or middle class, and homelessness is considered by many as the worst in the nation, with San Francisco so clogged with the bedraggled street people that visitors must be wary when walking the streets to avoid human waste. Meanwhile, these misguided socialists have classified that metropolis as a "Sanctuary City" as if they don't have enough mouths to feed. What has this done to the state's population? It has caused a mass migration estimated at more than four hundred citizens a day leaving the state. To be fair, plenty of young people are moving in as well, but most of these are well-educated individuals, technically qualified for the high-paying jobs in Silicon Valley. They make huge salaries and can afford the astronomical housing prices, but one has to wonder...where will they go to retire? That's easy to answer. Just look at the Northeast, where millions of Americans have worked for decades making big salaries and paying huge taxes. They are now retiring by the thousands every day and leaving New York to head for Florida or anywhere in the South where their retirement savings and pensions will survive with them to old age. These are just two examples of what a liberal America would look like, except that these people could ESCAPE the financial oppression of socialist liberalism and still be Americans. What if these people were in charge of our entire nation and economy? Think about this long and hard before you pull any lever in the next national election.

Further, one has to wonder. How does a robust economy affect a party whose platform seems aimed at the poor, unemployed, and hungry? Would a nation hard at work and earning a paycheck need them at all? Think about it.

The bottom line is...liberalism sounds good, but doesn't WORK!

CONFESSION

I am more worried about environmentalists than the environment.

grew up in a family dedicated to the exploration and delivery of
natural gas to American homes and businesses by means of pipelines,
which they spent their life laying across the nation from California
through Louisiana to New York. Their labors enabled me to live in a
comfortable house, go to school, and ultimately to attend college,
something few members of my family had ever done. But upon my
arrival at my college campus, I was immediately drawn to a movement
that convinced me that the planet was in imminent peril. I bought the
story hook, line and sinker. I bought the books and attended the
lectures. By the time I was nineteen, I was convinced that the planet
would collapse before I reached thirty, which would have been 1980!

I could stack those books up to my chin now, but their dire predictions are a distant memory. Their forecasts varied a bit from pundit to pundit, but the general prognostications included some elements of the following:

> The world would run out of oil within twenty-five years (1993).

> The internal combustion engine would be obsolete within twenty years (1988).

> The United States could not support a population of 200 million.

> The world could not support a population of 5 billion.

> Within twenty-five years (1993) the Western states would be wasteland...or a flooded plain.

> Within thirty years (1998) the United States would get virtually all its power from solar or windmills.

> If we didn't control population by 1980, people would be eating each other out of starvation.

These scientists were famous, respected, well educated, and unquestionably smart. They differed somewhat in their opinions, but they had one thing in common...they were all WRONG.

As I write this, the United States is supporting 330 million people. The world is getting by with 7 billion citizens. We have more oil in reserve now than we did in 1968. We have more natural gas than anybody ever thought possible. Solar and wind power are part of our energy grid, but it is an infinitesimal part of our energy usage.

My experience with experts who predict the end of the world has left me understandably cynical. I am one of those rare people who think when an expert predicts something, it ought to happen. If the weatherman predicts rain, I take an umbrella. If they predict snow, I buy a shovel. If my stockbroker predicts a stock to go up, I will buy some. If these forecasters fail consistently, I lose confidence in them and look elsewhere for information on which to base my decisions.

However, for some inexplicable reason, this rule doesn't seem to apply to many people today, especially young adults. Environmental scientists continue to issue cataclysmic predictions that don't arrive within their stated time frame. Many of these soothsayers have actually made a lifetime career out of issuing these dire warnings to the SAME audience for MORE THAN FORTY YEARS, who continue to hang on every word, even though not one of their predictions has come to pass! I find this incredible. Even Al Gore, a former vice president of the United States, got in on the act, producing a film "An Inconvenient Truth" that predicted (in 2006) that "seas could rise twenty feet in ten years." That was 2006. Fourteen years later, my favorite beach is still there! For this, he received a Nobel prize.

Let me make this perfectly clear. I "believe" in climate change. I am confident, in fact, that the climate is always changing. The history books are full of climatic changes, with massive shifts in temperature, snowfall, and storm activity. What I do NOT believe is that mankind, in just over one hundred years of industrialization, has modified this massive globe's weather to any significant degree. Further, I am convinced, regardless of the cause, that mankind is totally incapable of modifying the current or future weather patterns to any significant degree by buying electric cars or building windmills.

First of all, this planet runs on oil. It powers our cars, factories, airplanes, and ships at sea. It heats our homes and fuels our rockets into space. The effort to reduce our dependence on fossil fuels is admirable and worthy, but the idea that electricity and wind power are going to significantly reduce our need for petroleum-based fuels in the near future is folly.

For instance, every two minutes, twenty four hours a day, a jet airliner departs from Atlanta's Hartsfield-Jackson International Airport, filled with 200-300 passengers and more than 20,000 gallons of aircraft fuel (a 747 burns five gallons per MILE). This scene is repeated at airports all over the world, not to mention the thousands of ships and hundreds of military jets flying all over the world. There is NO alternative fuel existing today that could begin to replace petroleum in these applications, and any effort to eliminate oil production or use would paralyze the world's economy and bring international travel to a screeching halt.

Like most of the burning issues of the day, it is difficult to tell where genuine concern for our environment ends and political ambitions and strategies begin. Once you realize the far left's true agenda, it becomes increasingly obvious how easy that issues like single-payer government health care and environmental extremism could easily help advance their globalist goals. Eliminating oil production would cripple American industry, the military, and the nation's economy, but perhaps that is their goal, as strange as that may seem. When one closely examines their international environmental treaty initiatives, one cannot help but realize that these agreements clearly excuse major polluters like China and India while penalizing the United States. Then when you look at signatories to these treaties like Russia, who will likely never actually abide by the terms, one could only conclude that the only major power that will be required to comply is the United States.

The left has done a tremendous job of convincing many people (especially the young) that conservatives hate clean air and fresh water, or that we are so ignorant that we just don't see the crisis. Neither accusation is true. Where we differ is on the scope of the problem and how we go about improving the environment without destroying our country's economy and competitive position in the world. I believe that Donald Trump's refusal to sign the Paris "accord" may have saved our nation from a political and legal nightmare that would have lasted decades.

One of the many things that have been lost in this debate is how far we have come in the past sixty years, from an environmental standpoint. I grew up in the Northeast where the rivers like the Ohio and the Hudson were so polluted that fish couldn't survive and raw sewage flowed into the rivers unchecked. Factories spewed smoke from stacks, and cars emitted smoke from their tailpipes continuously. Today, automobiles emit virtually nothing into the atmosphere, the rivers flow cleanly, and smokestacks have all but disappeared. That is, in the United States.

Meanwhile, In Mexico City, '70s era Volkswagens puff their way through city streets where you can barely see three blocks but for the smog. In China, citizens wear facemasks to avoid the polluted air. In India, the rivers earn the distinction of the nastiest waterways on earth. It makes one wonder why, on the eve of the Paris accord, then-President Obama agreed to give China a twenty year pass on complying with the most critical covenants. Taking a look at this world scene, one has to conclude that every car owner in the United States could purchase a Prius or Tesla and it wouldn't make a dent in the earth's overall health.

Environmentalists and their friends in the media would have you believe that the majority of Americans believe the forecast of twenty-foot increases in ocean levels and impending doom. However, logic and observation makes this conclusion impossible. If the nations wealthy and educated believe the oceans are rising twenty feet in the next decade, then why is beachfront property still selling for millions?

Why are developers (with substantial financial backing) still building giant condos and shopping centers on the Miami waterfront within a stone's throw of the ocean? Why are celebrities still buying islands in the Caribbean? Why are millionaires still packing the Barrett-Jackson auto auction to pay hundreds of thousands of dollars for cars that require gasoline to operate? Why hasn't Richard Branson abandoned his private island...or at least starting sandbagging the shore line? For that matter, if the planet only has twelve years to live (as one freshman congresswoman has predicted) why are young adults even going to college? Why aren't coastal residents moving to higher ground? The only logical answer is that few people seriously believes this nonsense. It is part political strategy, part youthful activism and part group-think, which is the most powerful force in today's political arena.

So where does that leave this conservative? Am I proposing that we ignore our environment, burn down our forests, and pave the country with concrete? Of course not...I love this country and this planet as much as the next human. However, I accept that we must continue to improve our stewardship of this planet while still maintaining a healthy economy and strong military and produce enough food to allow us to survive and thrive. I would also propose that our efforts to stop real pollution begin with the countries that are doing the real polluting, starting with China and India, a process that could be much more easily achieved by real treaties that leverage political and economic sanctions that require reductions in pollution, rather than

toothless global "accords" that do little but scold the polluters an
cripple the U.S. economy.

Let me be clear. There is work to be done. We need to work to clean u
our oceans just as we did our rivers and streams fifty years ago. W
must explore and develop alternate power sources but NOT at th
expense of the progress of our nation by abandoning the fuel sourc
that is powering our economy. Further, we must all remember tha
"we" must include more than Americans buying electric cars an
paper straws. It must be a worldwide effort based on realisti
environmental goals, not political agendas.

The world is not coming to an end anytime soon. For anyone to mak
immediate political choices based on these doomsayers prediction
will only bring the demise of one region of this planet...ours!

CONFESSION

I Am Disgusted With The News Media.

I grew up in a world where "news" consisted of two sources: the daily newspaper that took about twenty-five minutes to read, and the evening news on network television that took about twenty-five minutes to watch after commercials. With those two data points, my father and most of America drew their conclusions about the state of world and national affairs, then decided the fate of the country and how they would vote in the next election.

No doubt, the news media of that era had a decidedly Democratic slant even then, but there was very little time for the newscasters of the day to inflect much political philosophy after reporting the real news of the day. That message was reserved for the national conventions, which my father watched with intense interest, even if they ran all night. A man who routinely went to bed at 8:30, he watched both conventions intently as he formed his opinion of each party's platform, which he assumed would accurately represent their actions once in office. Somehow, the nation survived for decades with this limited access to information; citizens like my father lived their lives, elected officials, built businesses, went to war, and raised families, all without a panel of experts to interpret the daily events and explain the long-term possible outcomes to every issue to an (apparently) ignorant and politically uninformed public.

Then, in 1980, a brilliant young entrepreneur named Ted Turner turned the information world upside down when he introduced a twenty-four-hour news channel called CNN. His ambition was noble. He figured that in a world with 6 billion people, there had to be more stories than just the latest forest fire or plane crash. He was right, and it was a brilliant idea, which was born out when the United States bombed Iraq in 1991. It was a twenty-four-hour fireworks show that transfixed Americans and catapulted CNN past the big three during the three-week assault.

His vision was legendary, and his goals were admirable, but sadly, they were largely unrealized. Instead of broadening their scope to international stories of people and events around the world in an educational and entertaining fashion, the network was soon hijacked by political forces who saw the non-stop invasion into American homes as an unavoidable opportunity to sway the electorate with highly biased stories twenty-four hours a day.

The birth of another network called FOX in 1996 probably cemented this shift to totally partisan storytelling, although it is hard to tell which came first, since it was sixteen years after the birth of CNN before FOX appeared on the air with a clearly conservative message. Both were preceded by the arrival of the Rush Limbaugh show, which first aired in 1984 in Sacramento, California, where he commanded an unprecedented three hours of air time almost totally devoid of music or on-air guests.

At any rate, the lines were clearly drawn, and soon the major networks (ABC, CBS, NBC)   followed suit with totally liberal agendas and twenty-four-hour companion cable stations. By now, any pretense that the networks were "just reporting the news" disappeared. Soon, citizens didn't just pick their political party; they chose their favorite news source. It became "news du jour" where liberals or conservatives could basically listen to the news they wanted to hear. Today's talk about "political division" cannot be blamed on Donald Trump. That ship sailed long ago. But there was a big difference (for me anyway) between the liberal mainstream and the new conservative networks. FOX news and Rush Limbaugh made no bones about their position....They were conservative and trying to balance what they saw as an extremely biased media. Meanwhile, (and to this day) the major networks project that they are the ultimate arbiters of truth.

At this point, any pretense of "journalistic integrity" went out the window. The mainstream media's bias to the Democratic Party became so blatant, it became (and remains) comical. From CNN providing allowing Donna Brazile to provide Hillary Clinton with debate questions to CBS's Sunday morning interviewing Hillary Clinton on the eve of her campaign while in the same show, introducing the star of the new series titled "Madam Secretary" about a blonde politician becoming Secretary of State. (How's that for subtle?) At this point, the networks went all-in without looking back.

Cataloging the hypocrisy and bias of the major network media would take so much space, I wouldn't know where to start. It occurs daily, hourly, minute by minute. I cannot watch fifteen minutes of the evening news without shaking my head. These pompous pundits can look straight into the camera and state the most ridiculous statements without so much as a smirk. They can report a story that they know is not true without a blink, even if the next day's events prove it a total fantasy.

And they do it in unison. While the average news consumer could reasonably assume that twenty different news organizations get up early every morning and gather raw information, then write their scripts independently, the facts speak otherwise. As one radio host regularly chronicles, by eight a.m. every morning, two dozen news organizations kick off their reports of the day with IDENTICAL verbiage, even down to the use of obtuse terms like "gravitas" which no one could possibly conjure up independently without being fed the days talking points from some central source.

he term "fake news" has become a favorite term from both political amps. Frankly, I am less concerned about "fake news" than I am "half-aked news," which I define as information that is fundamentally ccurate but ignores critical information, such as...

* The coverage of "Hands up...Don't shoot" that ignores the findings of an impartial grand jury that they never bothered to research.

* Criticizing the potential effect of tariffs on American products without mentioning that these tariffs don't apply to American-made goods, or to the possible benefit the tariffs might mean to American manufacturers, consumers and WORKERS.

* The report of a rumored liaison with a stripper by the current president after ignoring more than a DOZEN such accusations by women against Bill Clinton, including one who could provide a stained dress with DNA.

* Reports of "Russian collusion" without a single piece of evidence that even one vote was changed by this imaginary event.

* The coverage of the Hillary Clinton campaign without a single story about her near empty auditoriums or the massive rallies that gather at every Donald Trump appearance.

* The connection of Trump to "Charlottesville" although he had no connection to the event whatever, only a ham-fisted comment about the warring factions after the fact. To hear the evening news, Donald Trump was leading a charge holding a rebel flag.

* Reporting that the withdrawal of "troops" in the Middle Ea
  resulted in mass murder without detailing that this withdraw
  consisted of approximately fifty brave soldiers, not the battalior
  they inferred were involved.

* The coverage of Prince Andrew's association with Jeffrey Epstei
  while IGNORING the overwhelming evidence of former Presider
  Bill Clinton's long association with this pervert, including dozer
  of trips on the "Lolita Express" with Epstein to his private island
  with legions of underage girls in tow.

* Reporting that Trump was met with some "boos" from the crow
  at a fight in Madison Square Garden, but ignoring (and editing ou
  any coverage of the three-minute standing ovation from th
  102,000 fans attending the Alabama/LSU football game as he an
  the first lady arrived and were displayed on the jumbo-tron.

* Continuous coverage of the impeachment debacle without onc
  playing the video of Joe Biden threatening to withhold aid to th
  Ukraine unless they fired the prosecutor who investigated his sor
  Hunter, even though this clear act of "quid pro quo" strikes at th
  very heart of the impeachment issue. (I have liberal friends wh
  have never seen this video and don't even believe it exists!)

I could go on, but the evidence is there in living color each night on th
evening news and on the twenty-four-hour streaming cable "news
channels. "Reporters" who stare into the camera and read the day'
talking points without flinching, always predicting the imminent fall c

Donald Trump and the pending collapse of the nation if he is not removed.

I often wonder if the journalists sitting behind the desks on televised newscasts have any comprehension how they are viewed by citizens watching them from homes across the fruited plain as they condescend to them nightly, reporting story after story that eventually proves to be inaccurate or flat-out untrue. They obviously feel that these people are too ignorant to understand or remember the facts of the story. This arrogance has lowered public confidence in journalists to just above bill collectors and members of Congress. Yet they persist.

The same "group-think" environment that has gripped Hollywood, academia, and the scientific community has obviously taken total control of the major news media. I can only imagine what it is like for a young journalism major to arrive on their first day of employment at any of these institutions. It must become instantly apparent that their long-term success (or survival) depends on earning their stripes with the ability to create a sensational angle that will offset any positive news that might favor the right or a conservative president. After all, this is an industry that respects, above all else, one's ability to destroy a public figure or institution. Their heroes are Woodward and Bernstein, who brought down a president and won a Pulitzer Prize, a trophy that now commemorates those who can bring down the high and mighty, as long as their targets live on the "right" side of the street. The fact that this obvious bias toward one political philosophy with such a "scorched earth, take no prisoners" approach mirrors the actions of Joseph McCarthy and his minions, seems lost on a generation who barely remembers 9/11. Furthermore, it is clear that, like McCarthy, they are certain that the enemy is so objectionable that any tactics are justified. From my perspective, the same sins are being committed but by the other side, who seem oblivious to the long-term damage they are doing to real freedom and democracy.

The saddest element of the present state of "journalism" is the absolute absence of any understanding of what the profession even means. As I mentioned earlier, my first job was writing obituaries and short features for an old-fashioned, hard core editor. I never completed the shortest, most insignificant story that I did not get summoned to his office where I was raked over the coals for the most minor errors. "Babies are held...meetings are CONDUCTED!" he would bellow. "Sheep go over fences. Budgets are EXCEEDED," he would continue. I sat at my typewriter shaking as I typed, but I learned to get things RIGHT. Now, every morning, I review the news online, and I find three typos before I finish the first story, even from national news services. This is not to mention the total absence of sentence structure, grammar, or syntax. Clearly, a generation who grew up typing a grammatically fractured message in a text is now in charge of our news media.

Watching the evening news or cable news networks actually saddens me. It is distinctly clear that the folks at CNN and MSNBC are so focused on destroying our duly elected president that they feel any distortion or omission of facts is justified because their goal is so just and urgent. However, they are oblivious to the damage they are doing to their profession, to the electoral process, and to our government's ability to rule effectively. It is unmistakably evident to me that they KNOW that the information they are broadcasting is inaccurate, even though this act runs counter to everything the journalism profession stands for.

It is this assumption that the "ends justify the means" that fueled Joe McCarthy to ruin the lives and careers of hundreds of Americans in the desire to eradicate communism. What Joe missed, and what today's media are overlooking, are two key elements:

1. The First Amendment of our Constitution protects ALL speech and philosophy, regardless of its source or content.

2. If one political message is superior to another, it will become self-evident by its execution, and the voters will choose the better product without depressing anyone's message.

It is precisely these undeniable facts that horrify the media and the leadership of the liberal Democratic movement. They know they cannot sell their socialistic, globalist, government-controlled system without distorting the facts of their plans and objectives. Down South, we call that "putting lipstick on a pig."

Sadly, true journalism appears to be dead.

CONFESSION

The Conservative Position Requires a Lot of Sacrifice

I love music. I love art. I love the theater. And for forty years, I have enjoyed these pursuits with a passion. In the seventies and eighties, my wife and I spent every weekend at concerts. We saw the Stones when they were young...The Eagles, Linda Ronstadt, Bob Dylan, Willie Nelson, Doobie Brothers, Randy Newman, John Prine, Bonnie Raitt...I could go on. Music was, and is, an essential part of our life. The artists were perfecting their craft and performing without political lectures.

Likewise, We have enjoyed "Saturday Night Live" since its inception, from Belushi's killer bees to Dan Aykroyd's Coach Ditka. Saturday night was reserved for the show, and all our friends gathered round as we partied. That all continued until about ten years ago when the entire entertainment industry decided it was their job to promote the alues of the Democratic Party and insult anyone who wasn't on board. This was a problem for me, since I am one who expects entertainers, whom I have paid 400 bucks to see, to display their talents, not lecture me with issues they know little about. Thus, I can no longer attend concerts or watch late-night TV, afternoon talk shows, award shows like the Oscars, where a political speech has become required, or even the Super Bowl half-time show, which has become a political "football" (sorry) where certain celebrities are criticized in advance for accepting an invitation to perform or failing to include a "message" encoded in their presentation. For God's sake, is a football game!

fascinating thing happens when young people with a special talent singing, acting, playing guitar) suddenly achieve some success and notoriety, then arrive on the scene in Hollywood. As if by osmosis, they instantly become experts in politics, environmental science, international relations, and global economics. It is incredible. Equally amazing is the reaction by millions of fans who hang on their every word as these overnight Svengalis speak of current events as if they held a master's degree on the subject at hand, even though many of them barely finished high school. This is just one element of the dangers of "group speak," this version born out this nation's fixation with fame, even if the celebrity of note is often a college dropout or social misfit who has been bankrupt, divorced twice, and attended rehab repeatedly. For me, taking political or environmental guidance from Ted Danson is like taking financial advice from Wilford Brimley.

The saddest part of this insulting debacle is that many of these "experts" actually think they are moving Americans to their point of view. From my observation, this could not be further from the truth. The Americans I observe are disgusted with this invasion of their entertainment choices and their values. The decision for some celebrities to take a political stance is not new and, in and of itself, admirable. When Marlon Brando refused his Academy Award and sent a Native American to represent him, I saw it as a heartfelt expression of his personal view. But today, this need to include a left-wing political message with every performance, every appearance, every award acceptance speech has become an industry requirement to remain in the "Club," which carries with it a requirement that the celebrity's position be decidedly liberal. Clearly, any young star who would dare take a public stand that was conservative would be shunned outright and online, then run out of Tinseltown before the week was out. If there is any doubt, simply look at the events that unfolded after Ellen Degeneres made the monumental mistake of simply being PHOTOGRAPHED sitting with George W. Bush, a former president of the United States. Ellen, an established A-lister, was nearly ruined by simply SITTING with an individual who represented an unpopular position, at least to the liberal tribe for which she is a major icon.

Most ironic to me when observing this new "our way or the highway" position and political movement is that it flies in the face of a critical historic event that most liberals consider the most prejudicial and discriminatory moment in the history of Hollywood, that being the

McCarthy hearings on communism and the subsequent blackballing of major actors, producers, writers, and producers simply for their personal political beliefs. This campaign ruined these professionals' lives and careers in a lengthy inquisition that violated the First Amendment and the freedoms that I thought we all held dear and that we would not again sacrifice in the name of politics.

But even a glance at today's atmosphere in Hollywood would cause any informed observer to conclude that we have entered an era of "Reverse McCarthyism," where only one position is tolerated and all others are demonized and condemned. Like an angry crowd surrounding the gallows, this inquisition builds both a collective anger in the industry as a group and fear in individuals that any effort to question this crucifixion might mean adding them to the execution lineup. Just ask any conservative (or Christian) celebrity, from Tim Tebow, Paula Deen, and Roseanne, to the folks on Duck Dynasty, the Duggars, or even a major rap star like Kanye West.

All of this hysteria might not be possible without the advent of social media and programs like Twitter. Within seconds of the televised image of Ellen sitting with George W. Bush, the internet exploded with attacks on this popular talk show host, even though she had not spoken, expressed an opinion, or even a physical connection (read: hug) with this demonic figure. Again, I am baffled why some semblance of logic or rational thought cannot prevail. What does 300,000 tweets really mean? What if it were 1 million? There are 330 million people in this country. Can a collection of misspelled messages from totally anonymous trolls dominate the national conversation? This is insane.

I applaud Hollywood for trying to lead the national conversation. However, I wish that they would take a serious look at how their actions are affecting the principles our nation was founded on, like free speech and free assembly. Someone, perhaps Ellen herself, needs to call a time-out. Clearly, the entertainment industry has to realize that they are fostering the same atmosphere of intolerance that they have so long protested. After all, if you are so confident in your values, how can a conflicting position harm yours? People should look at their options and choose the superior position. That is how our country is supposed to work.

Perhaps, they could look to the actions and opinions of the stars of the classic era. Actors that served in the military, died in service, toured the world to entertain the troops...names like Jimmy Stewart, Bob Hope, Henry Fonda, Charlton Heston, Paul Newman, Steve McQueen, and Rock Hudson, all of whom served honorably in World War II. The names of classic film and recording stars who served in that war is lengthy and star-studded, with more than a few who died in service, including Guy Lombardo and Carole Lombard. God forbid that our nation's freedom would depend on the service and support of today's celebrities in film, music, or sports. I wonder sometimes if the past forty years has not just been some sort of fools paradise where two generations have grown up and old without the first threat to their personal safety or prosperity. I hope that status holds up, but it cannot stand without solid support of our military and our soldiers.

In the meantime, if our Hollywood stars refuse to support our country and its leadership, I will be unable to support or enjoy their talents. I will miss them. I hope they miss me!

CONFESSION

I Am Opposed to National Free Health Care

Let me be clear, I like free stuff! But over the years, I have learned that very few "free" things in the world arrive without a price to be paid somewhere. Three months of "free" HBO comes with a one-year contract at $19.95 a month. A free service from an online website allows them to sell my name and personal information. And when politicians offer something free, I really start to wonder where the hook is hidden.

With federally funded "free" health care, the hook is obvious to me, since it is being promoted by a party that wants to create a "nanny state" wherein citizens are dependent upon the U.S. government for their very existence, although I believe their motivation goes much deeper. As I have stated several times, I am convinced that the liberal emocratic leadership's ultimate goal is to create a nation state where powerful few control everything the populace wears, eats, drives, rinks, or smokes. There can be no easier method to accomplish this 1an by controlling health care. Think about it…what can you name 1at is not affected by or does not affect your health? Nothing. From our living room carpet (chemicals and dyes) and air conditioner PVCs and freon), to your clothes (dyes) and backyard garden pesticides) you cannot name a single object or activity whose use annot be linked to your health. Everything from the food you eat and 1e plates you use to your choice of prenatal care and the design of our child's car seat have some effect on your overall health. What is vrong with that? Plenty. Let us suppose that we install a single payer ederal health care and everything is FREE. Hurray! Just wait a few ears until the government starts compiling statistics. Suddenly, there ; a report that head injuries from football are "costing" $200 million a ear, which is being paid by taxpayers. Or that sugar is causing obesity nd costing "taxpayers" a billion dollars a year. Remember my story bout salt in the restaurant? The liberal solution was to take it away. Vith the federal government paying for all the medical costs, it would nly seem prudent to curtail these activities and products that are reating these health crises, right? Then we have to get into deciding vho gets health care and when. As we all know, if it is free, everyone vill be going in for every hangnail. Not to mention the several million aby boomers (who are largely conservative) that will be clogging up 1e system as they get older. Add the left's obsession with patient-ssisted suicide, and you have a prescription for disaster.

Of course, the legislators pondering this thorny subject will all get their health care free regardless, along with their congressional or senatorial salaries for life. Do you want these people in charge of your health care? Please understand, I am not a fan of health insurance companies, but I like them better than politicians. Further, I believe strongly in the free market and would rather corporate America run this business and employ private citizens to work in it. Likewise, I would love to see that every legal citizen has access to basic health care. I just cannot abide by the concept of our government controlling the purse strings and the eligibility.

All this aside, I cannot imagine the graft and inefficiency of the government running such a national institution. The Medicare system is already mired in fraud and abuse by nursing homes, unscrupulous doctors, clinics, drug companies, home care assistance companies and medical supply providers. A national health care system would sink us financially. I have spent the last twenty years providing for aging relatives, primarily my mother (who passed not long ago at age 96) and my mother-in-law who will turn 94 in 2020. I have observed first-hand the blatant abuse and overbilling practices of health care providers, regardless of the age of the patient. I believe that the first step toward reducing fraud and abuse would be federal legislation that requires all medical service providers to issue an itemized invoice to ANY patient (or their caregiver) for any and all services rendered regardless of what institution is paying the bill. As it is, most Americans walk in and out of a medical facility with little concern about the cost as long as "somebody else" is footing the bill, whether that "someone" is the government, their insurer, or their union. I strongly believe that if citizens, regardless of their political affiliation, began to see the bills for $80 Band-aids and $50 aspirins, it would have an immediate and measurable effect on health care care costs. Why hasn't this been initiated already? That question is easy to answer...because the health care lobby is so strong as to block any legislation that would pull back the curtain on this unmonitored gravy train. This is an issue that affects ALL Americans and that ALL Americans could support if they had a chance. But you will notice that this is not a part of the national political conversation because politicians don't want you to see the real issues, the real adversaries, the real problems, and the real potential solutions.

This is also another example of the value of Donald Trump. He has proposed just such legislation, like requiring drug makers to list the actual cost of drugs on TV ads, and this is the real reason the Washington establishment is obsessed with removing him from office ..because he is UPSETTING THE ESTABLISHMENT APPLECART in every sector of our government.

As I write this, our president is under inquiry for a policy known as "Quid Pro Quo," meaning the effort of a politician to require some individual, industry, or country to provide some goods or service for legislative action. That any Washington politician could accuse anyone else of this policy is outrageous, if not laughable. Washington runs on "Quid Pro Quo" twenty-four hours a day. It could not function without it...from federal subsidies for dairy farmers to government contracts to military suppliers for planes and electronics, "Quid Pro Quo" defines the nature of every government transaction and has since the dawn of this nation.

But I digress. Just trust me, you do not want these political demagogues running the entire health care system, and remember this, once you let this hungry cat loose, you will NEVER get it back in the bag. In the history of this great nation, no government program of this magnitude has ever been repealed once in place, with the exception of President Trump's effort to halt the "Affordable Care Act." A single-payer federal health care system is a one-way ticket to socialism with a taxpayer price tag that will change this country, our economy, and our future FOREVER.

Look before you leap, and think before you vote.

CONFESSION

I Am Very Concerned about Violence in Our Country

I grew up in a very rural part of Southern Ohio. Every house I visited had a shotgun sitting by the back door and a pistol on the nightstand of the parents' bedroom. No background checks, no permits, no trigger locks. My elementary school held square dances and PTA events where they raffled off shotguns or rifles for fundraising. Guns were sold everywhere (without permits or background checks) from Sears and Montgomery Ward to Western Auto. Gunfire could routinely be heard from my house, but it was target shooters or hunters. No one ever shot up a school, church, or theater. Pickup trucks in my high school parking lot had gun racks in their cabs. Real gun violence originated with a crazy husband, a career criminal, or a suicide.

In 1966, we heard the news of a young man climbing the clock tower at the University of Texas, where he began shooting people at random, killing fourteen and wounding thirty-four others. He was angry at his parents, the military, and the college. Everyone chalked it up as a freak incident, and for almost forty years, that was the correct conclusion. Until 1999, when two high school students at Columbine High School in Colorado barricaded themselves in their school, then proceeded to kill twelve students, shoot twenty-one others, a teacher and themselves for no apparent reason. Since then, mass shootings have become alarmingly routine. This has prompted groups across the country to take action to prevent further such occurrences. This is certainly understandable. I know of no one who does not wish to take action to prevent such massacres. However, many of these well-meaning activists are solely focused on removing the weapons as the solution to the problem.

For me, this presents a challenge to logic and common sense. I have researched the details of mass shootings from Columbine to the present, and I have seen an obvious trend. The majority of these shooters have three things in common...they are predominantly young, white, and male. The idea that the combination of young white men and guns must equal mass violence flies in the face of one obvious fact...this country has contained copious numbers of young white men and guns since the arrival of the Mayflower. Yet these pointless massacres only began about twenty years ago. Obviously, some other forces must be at work here. For me, it raises the question: what societal changes have occurred since 1999 that would cause young en to indiscriminately murder their friends and classmates without

eason?

/hat has happened in the world since 1999 that would change young

eople's attitudes about their fellow humans?

decided to make a list...

VIOLENT VIDEO GAMES. For some time, we have had video games that simulate the killing of humans to such a degree that it is indiscernible from a real killing. It is estimated now that a serious gamer has "killed" more than a million people by the age of sixteen. Game fans discount this influence, but how can it not affect a young person's view of fellow human beings?

SOCIAL MEDIA. In virtually every case of bullying or suicide in a public school, administrators list social media as a major cause of the conflict that lead to the ultimate event. Obviously, this communication tool is here to stay, but it has to be considered when trying to find the source of the anger and despair that lead to these violent events. I am not a child psychologist or behavioral scientist but I have had the opportunity to observe the effects of social media on children of friends and relatives. It has led me to an inescapable conclusion..that while most of us look upon our classmates from years past as old friends, many of today's students now look upon the school environment as a sea of bullies and cliques that have made their school experience a minefield of enemies, not friends. I sincerely believe that this is the SINGLE BIGGEST CAUSE of Columbine type attacks in the recent years. Removing guns from society (which will be nearly impossible) may reduce the body count but not the source of the problem. This is a SERIOUS CRISIS that is affecting our entire society especially when you consider that when these children grow up, many go out into the world with the same fear, anger and distrust of the world around them.

ELECTRONIC ISOLATION. Not too long ago, a roomful of young people meant a noisy group of individuals shouting and talking to one another. Today it means a silent group of zombies staring into phones and typing with their thumbs. Add the 3-D headgear and you have silent statues who cannot even see each other, much less interact with one another. Lack of interaction between all strata of our society can only lead to more violence and less respect for fellow humans.

VIOLENT ENTERTAINMENT. While network and Hollywood producers express their dismay about gun violence, they continue to produce shows and movies that are full of explosions, machine guns, personal warfare, torture, and total destruction of property. This is especially true when you look at movies developed to attract the exact demographic that describes our assassins...young men. The typical action movie blows up three buildings, wrecks two cars, kills a half dozen humans, and unloads a thousand rounds of machine gun ammo before the opening credits. Then, when they are not shooting or torturing someone, they are elevating vampires and zombies to human status, thus creating more distance between fantasy and reality.

This social disconnect typifies the media's position on firearms. On talk shows and news specials like "60 Minutes," the case is frequently made that we should eliminate all firearms completely, but in primetime, the story shifts dramatically. For instance, CBS shows like Sunday Morning frequently feature editorial monologues that plead for someone to "Do Something" to end gun violence. These pleadings are heart-wrenching, but I can't help wondering why CBS doesn't "Do Something" by leading the way and removing all handguns and automatic weapons from their evening lineup to show us what a world without guns looks like. That shouldn't be too difficult. All they would have to do is cancel or revamp Blue Bloods, NCIS, NCIS New Orleans, Criminal Minds, FBI Most Wanted, FBI, SEAL Team, SWAT, Magnum PI, and Hawaii Five-O. Plus the gun-toting favorites on their classics channel, which includes everything from Flashpoint, the Guardian, Gunsmoke, JAG, MacGyver, to Jericho, Mission Impossible, and Nash Bridges...just to name a few. Don't hold your breath. In the world of liberal leadership, it is "do as I say, not as I do" as they drive their massive SUVs, build 25,000-square-foot mansions and surround themselves with armed guards and their property with ten-foot walls.

ONLINE PORNOGRAPHY. There is nothing new about young men (or women) viewing pornography, but the context has changed drastically. Until the birth of the internet, the images were static, difficult to access, and easy for adults to monitor. Today, high definition video is a click away, is available on any device, and it is impossible to monitor. For young men and women, these unrealistic portrayals of sexual relations to pubescent teenagers is extremely dangerous. It portrays unrealistic body images of men and women, and acts that pervert the adolescent sexual learning curve. This process is supposed to be a gradual journey of experimentation and exploration, not a sudden, overwhelming attack on innocent minds and ever-changing bodies. The full effect that this brand new media is having on our children is immeasurable, but the damage being done is obvious. Once again, it is too late to put this digital genie back in the bottle, but it may not be too late to do something about it.

ABSENCE OF FAITH. I am not naive enough to suggest that we can heal our children's anger and despair by sending them all to Sunday School, but I firmly believe that all human beings benefit when they develop a sincere faith in a power greater than themselves and the institutions that surround them. For me, my belief in God served as a final gut-check when I faced a moral decision without a parent or teacher around to consult. Did I still do wrong? Certainly, but I knew it was wrong when I did it. Today, you must ask yourself...who is really teaching our children right from wrong? Most parents are too busy, and the schools are not even allowed to try. The church and organizations like the Scouts represent the last bastion of hope for instilling a personal moral compass in every child as they grow and mature, which should make you wonder why the liberal establishment is so determined to destroy these organizations. I guess faith in the government is all they feel is necessary.

LACK OF HEROES. Everybody needs heroes, especially young people...brave individuals known for their dedication and accomplishments. These days, real heroes are hard to find. In the past fifteen years, the closest thing we have had to a real hero was a pilot who crashed his plane in the Hudson River. Don't get me wrong, Sully's actions were truly heroic, but what happened to the guys who kept their craft aloft while they crossed the Atlantic like Lindbergh or to the moon and back like Neil Armstrong and crew? Where are our sports heroes? Don't look to ESPN for answers. In 2015, they awarded the Arthur Ashe "Courage" award to Bruce "Caitlyn" Jenner. And what act of heroism did this former Olympian achieve to win this historic award? "She" got a sex change. As I write this, the sports industry's major hero is Colin Kaepernick, heralded by Nike for disrespecting the flag and national anthem.   Wow! These people may be heroes, but doesn't it seem like our bar for heroism is getting pretty low?

ABSENCE OF DISCIPLINE. In a recent college football game between Clemson and Louisville, a defensive player attacked an opposing player while he was on the ground, punching him in the face for no apparent reason. At this point, Clemson Coach Dabo Swinney charged onto the field before the referee even had time to throw a penalty flag, admonishing his own player, and sending him to the locker room. He followed up this action by placing the offending player on a public bus to ride 450 miles home while the team took a one hour flight by air. "[He] has responded well," Swinney said. "He is disappointed in himself, embarrassed. He has apologized to our team and our AD. He's been extremely remorseful. What happened is way out of character for who he is. Very pleased with how he has taken ownership. He had a long bus ride home last night and plenty of time to think about it." That is what discipline is all about but it is sadly absent from most corners of our society. For several thousand years, parental discipline included the option of giving one's child a tap on the backside (as I experienced both at school and at home) when nothing else worked. Then, about twenty years ago, liberals campaigned to end this barbaric practice, stating that "corporal punishment" was child abuse and that ending this custom would end the "cycle of violence." I must ask...how did that work out? Today, we have the most violent and disrespectful children in this nation's history. Does this give those liberals reason to reflect? Of course not. The concept of "cause and effect" is lost on them.

could list dozens of critical societal shifts that have occurred in the past two decades, but these key factors help illustrate the point that I feel must be considered in analyzing why these young people have suddenly become killers without any logical basis. All of these new influences share one thing in common...they all serve to desensitize and de-personalize fellow humans in the minds of the young people who have lived a lifetime in a fantasy world. Kids no longer see their fellow humans as flesh-and-blood entities, just avatars and Facebook icons. Their conversations are no longer face to face but typed into an abbreviated text or a message copied to a couple hundred others they barely know. When insults are delivered (as they surely will,) they will not be shouted into a person's face but in a snarky two-line post that includes half their peers in the conflict. No wonder the suicide rate of children is the highest in the nation's history.

Anyone who thinks the problem of teen suicides and mass shootings will be solved by outlawing guns is delusional. What we have here is not a gun problem, but an anger problem, a social problem, a mental health issue that is affecting everyone from depressed teens to disenchanted former employees, divorcing spouses, and struggling veterans returning from service. People do not need guns to commit acts of violence. They can, and do, kill and maim others with cars, explosives, knives, poison, and as we learned on 9/11, airplanes. What we need to do is ask ourselves WHY this is happening? Then we need to make a national, non-partisan effort to answer this question.

I would challenge anyone reading this to conduct an exercise. Go dow
to your local library and look in the newspaper archives of your loca
paper for the news thirty years ago. Study a week's worth of the loca
and national events, then compare it to a week of today's news. Th
comparison is STARTLING. Those old papers will chronicle a the
here, an assault there, or a fight at a local bar. Today, a week's worth o
news in my hometown of 100,000 people includes a shooting ever
day, a sexual assault every day, a report of teacher having sex with
student somewhere every day, and most disturbing, a report of
public official (school principal, councilman, or deputy sheriff
trafficking in child pornography EVERY DAY.

Deciding to solve these problems by outlawing guns is just laz
thinking; 99.9 percent of the gun owners in this country have neve
shot another human being or been involved in any type of senseles
violence. Taking away guns to end gun violence would be lik
outlawing cars to save 50,000 lives that are lost every year i
accidents. It might be effective, but it is not solving the core problem.
and it will NEVER happen.

Further, this conservative has to wonder why liberal Democrats are s
focused on this one solution rather than seeking a real answer. It is m
sincere belief that this issue, like all others, is simply a means to a
end. To achieve a socialist, globalist state that seeks to manage th
nation's populace with sticks and carrots (like free healthcare,)
would be absolutely necessary to disarm the citizenry first. A tru
socialist society requires several elements, among them total contr

by the state, removal of wealth by private citizens, and elimination of any organized opposition.

Bottom line...ending violence by outlawing guns would be like solving obesity by outlawing spoons.

CONFESSION

I Oppose Abortion in All but the Most Extreme Circumstances

I once knew a young couple. He was eighteen, she was seventeen, and they had little that would lead anyone to conclude that they were prepared to raise a child and build a family. He had no job and little education or trade. She was in high school, and they had no money or prospects. However, their families joined together to develop a plan. Both families were devout Southern Baptists, and the word "abortion" never entered the conversation. This couple's prospects were bleak and future doubtful at best, but they married, he found a job, and they rented a small apartment. A beautiful baby followed soon, and time passed quickly. They enjoyed their life and grew together.

I still see this couple every day, in the mirror and at breakfast, since it is the story of me and my wife. We have been married fifty blissful years without a minute's regret. That baby we could have "terminated" grew up, became an outstanding athlete, student, graduate of college and graduate school, and an award-winning educator who lives five minutes from us. She has been a public school administrator for twenty-six years and touched the lives of more than 50,000 elementary and middle school students in this community. I can't imagine what my world and the world around us would have been if she had not been part of it. She has been a joy to my family and to everyone around her since the day she was born.

I realize that not all of life's stories end this way, (although it is difficult to see the ending of a story if it has no beginning) but I feel it is critical to give each life a chance, even if the situation seems hopeless at the time. There are so many options available today to solve the issues of the mother AND the child.

When asked, I often say that I am "pro-choice" on this issue. By that I mean that every individual has a choice as to whether they engage in sex, when, where, and under what circumstances they choose to do so. And if they wish to make this critical move, they have a plethora of birth control options available to avoid pregnancy, and if a pregnancy occurs, there are a multitude of options for allowing this child to live and survive, starting with the thousands of willing and qualified potential parents waiting for a baby to adopt.

I realize that this is a subject with some thorny, gender-based elements. When pregnancy occurs, it is the female who bears the decisions, the pain, and the life-altering circumstances that will affect her, regardless of the decisions made, and this is not fair. We now have DNA by which we can definitely determine the identity of the father, and I would support legislation that places serious penalties or financial responsibilities on the father, something that should have been in place years ago, a liability that should not require the mother to take legal action to set in motion.

There is another chapter to the story of the happy couple chronicled above. About five years after the birth of our first child, my wife became seriously ill. Normally in perfect condition, she became fatigued and listless. A series of doctors could find nothing wrong, so we traveled to Birmingham, Alabama, for our annual Thanksgiving feast. Later that night, she was uncharacteristically tired, so she went to bed early in the evening as the family continued to celebrate the holiday. Finally, around 11 p.m., I went into the guest room to check on her, where I found her cold and lifeless with blue lips and no pulse. Luckily, Brookwood Hospital was five minutes away, so her brother and I packed her into the car while the family called the facility. Emergency room staff met us with a gurney outside and a unit of blood for each arm, which they encased in blood pressure cuffs to force the flow. She was taken directly to surgery while we worked on obtaining more blood, since her type is AB-Negative, virtually the world's rarest type. Ultimately, she needed eight units in a surgery that lasted for what seemed like forever. Finally, the surgeons appeared to tell us that she was alive and would survive. They explained that she had experienced an "ectopic pregnancy" where an gg is fertilized in the fallopian tubes but cannot develop further. This aused the internal bleeding that almost cost her life. The fetus could ever have been brought to term, but, nonetheless, it gave me a ersonal and permanent understanding that there are circumstances here a pregnancy must be ended for the life of the mother, especially hen there is no hope for the developing fetus.

ly ultimate position on the subject of abortion is one that will not lease anyone on either side on this emotional issue. Reluctantly, I can ccept the painful decision of ending a pregnancy in the first trimester ue to extreme circumstances, such as rape, incest, or medical threat o the mother where no other solution is possible. However, I can find o reasonable excuse for not taking this drastic step within the first inety days. I find elective abortion morally wrong but as a strict onstitutionalist, I can only tolerate this amendment and hope we can mit its consequences as much as possible.

he current efforts of liberals to allow abortion in full-term regnancies is not only unacceptable, but immoral and disgusting. Vhat possible justification could any person provide to explain this nmerciful and cruel act of depravity? The fact that the liberal wing of he Democratic Party (is there another one?) considers this one of heir goals says a lot about this party's priorities. I find this attitude ppalling.

he Fourteenth Amendment to the Constitution legalized abortion in 973. I have always opposed this legislation, but at this point, I am more concerned about how far these extremists want to take this law than the law itself. As I have said earlier, I have reluctantly accepted the reality that some individuals in dire situations may find this the only solution (although I reject the idea that there are not better remedies available.) Today, however, I see a major shift in public opinion even in the youngest, child-bearing citizens, because of one very significant scientific event that has changed the pregnancy process irrevocably. Thirty years ago, couples and their families stood around the delivery room (with gender based cigars in hand) waiting for the announcement of the birth and the gender of the newborn. The advent of the ultrasound changed all of that forever. Now, young couples anticipate that first unveiling in a doctor's office as soon as eight weeks, when they see their baby and realize that it is a viable human being that belongs to them, and that any effort to end that pregnancy will end a life they created. I honestly believe that, if the ultrasound had been in widespread use in 1973, there would have never been a Fourteenth Amendment.

I wish every child could be recognized for the miracle that it is, and could be. Who knows, the child may be the next Einstein!

CONFESSION

I Find the Current Debate over Immigration Baffling

Our country is roughly 300 years old, depending on how you do your calculations. During that time, we have always maintained some limits on immigration, for the sake of population control, disease prevention, and the blocking of terrorist and other undesirables (not to be confused with deplorables.) But as I write these words, some members of one political party are promoting the concept of "open borders," apparently pushing for a country where there is absolutely no control of our borders, our population, or the quality of the immigrants entering our nation. Oddly, when these proponents extol the virtues of this concept, they are almost always displaying a photo or video of the Statue of Liberty, followed by one of the Mexican border, not the incoming gate at LaGuardia airport, where I assume they are still requiring passports and visas to enter.

As a strict constitutionalist, I oppose this concept totally. But as a fiscal conservative, I can't help but look at the "open borders" idea as a potential budget windfall if this idea ever becomes law. After all, when it comes to freedom and equality, I believe in freedom for EVERYONE, not just those crossing the Mexican border or immigrants who could potentially become new voters for the Democratic Party. So, if the open borders policy has any chance of becoming law, I propose that we go whole hog. Here is what "open borders" means to me...

ELIMINATION OF THE IMMIGRATION DEPARTMENT. Why would we need an agency to control borders we consider open? This would mean the elimination of 26,000 government jobs and the budget savings of $3.2 BILLION.

REPEAL OF ALL IMMIGRATION LAWS. If we have open borders, why would we need laws to control them?

ELIMINATION OF THE PASSPORT/VISA DEPARTMENT. Again, if we have open borders, why would we need any passes to enter?

ELIMINATION OF CENSUS DEPARTMENT AND CENSUS. If we open the borders and allow immigrants to enter without control, then obtain federal and state benefits, vote in our elections, what is the point of counting citizens when we don't know who or where they are? And it would save us a ton of money...the 2020 Census is estimated to cost $15.6 BILLION.

Since we already have an estimated fifteen million illegal residents, this exercise seems pointless.

ELIMINATION OF ALL CENSUS-BASED GOVERNMENT ALLOCATIONS. Thousands of government programs are based on population density and location. With no control of immigration or information on the location of citizens, how can we possibly allocate funds with inaccurate population information?

Does this make sense to you? No? Me either. But this is the kind of illogical nonsense it takes for any reasonably intelligent person to support an open border policy. Now, perhaps you can see why I am baffled. No rational, intelligent person can possibly support the idea of simply opening the gates to our nation without so much as registering them in some fashion and initiating temporary or permanent citizenship. Frankly, I honestly don't think the politicians pushing this concept actually plan to officially undertake this policy except for the southern border, a selective program that (as I have illustrated above) is illogical, impractical, and dangerous. Any official legislative effort would require the very steps I have outlined, a step that would mean welcoming potential terrorists into New York City, the home of the worst domestic terrorist attack in U.S. history, a move that no voter of any party is going to support if they are presented the concept as I have presented it here.

For the many kind-hearted liberals who see this as a "humanitarian crisis" that will be solved by total elimination of national borders, it is truly unfortunate that they cannot realize that this is simply a political gambit by a party that cannot exist or succeed without a steady stream of victims who believe that their very existence is dependent upon the Democratic Party, which is why it is critical that their "open borders" concept includes immediate qualification to vote without so much as a voter registration card. The Democratic Party knows that the country is conservative at its heart and that they can only prevail if they can continuously replenish their supply of voting blocks that feel their freedom is dependent on one party and threatened by another.

Essential to this strategy is maintaining the idea that conservative Republicans oppose immigration simply out of hatred based on race. This is ludicrous, but they are doing a great job of selling this position. Speaking for this conservative, I can state unequivocally that I welcome these newcomers with open arms, just as my great grandparents (from Germany and Ireland) were welcomed a hundred years ago. However, my ancestors came ashore, registered their arrival, studied the language, and embraced our culture, our language, and our flag. I expect nothing less of our new visitors from the south. I just want them to respect and obey our laws. After all, what kind of relationship can we build with an individual whose first act upon arriving here is an illegal one?

It is important to note that this is not a process I have been watching from my easy chair, like many northeasterners do as they watch the

esperate river crossings across the Rio Grande on the evening news. I
ave lived in North Carolina for thirty-five years, and I have observed
1e Mexican migration first hand since they first started arriving in
ur state about twenty years ago. Like most Carolinians, I was
npressed with their work ethic and ambition. These people work
ARD, they are dependable, and they take pride in their craft. They
ok over virtually all of the labor-intensive skilled industries, from
ouse painting, roofing, carpentry, and heavy construction.

nitially, they worked for existing contractors who paid them a decent
ut minimal wage, but they soon began opening their own firms and
iring their own crews, thus experiencing the American dream as
nmigrants have done for generations. Now, these Hispanic
ewcomers are an essential part of our state's culture and economy.

Ve welcome these people...We just want them to live here legally! Is
nat too much to ask?

CONFESSION

I Am very disappointed in the state of race relations today

I watched the civil rights movement live and in person. I was teenager in the sixties and the vision of African Americans marchin and getting attacked in the streets was eye-opening, to say the least. grew up in a totally white world. The teachers were white, the polic were white, the faces on TV were white. In fact, until I was 18, the onl black people I had seen were shining shoes or picking cotton and I ha to travel down south or to large urban area to see either. But as entered college and began to see the world in a broader view, th injustice of the racial divide became obvious. It wasn't about slaver anymore, it wasn't about the civil war or Abraham Lincoln. It was th clear realization that black Americans had been treated as secon class citizens (or non-citizens) for almost a hundred years after the had been "freed."

I listened to Martin Luther King and was spellbound. Then I watched as the nation and our leaders came forth with a flurry of legislation and initiatives that I felt sure would end this injustice in a generation. And as I grew older, that seemed to be the reality. People of color were admitted, by law, into virtually every organization, college, workplace, business and public space. It seemed that the problem had been solved and the world would be right at last. Soon, people of all races were living side by side, attending the same colleges, shopping at the same stores and living together in peace.

If someone had told me in 1970 that we would still be experiencing conflict over the color of one's skin in 2020, I would have called them insane. But here we are, 50 years later, still experiencing conflict and prejudice, all based on the amount of melanin in people's skin. Frankly, by the year 2000, I thought we would be past the whole issue. Then we elected the first black President, which I thought would be the turning point to total racial harmony. But it wasn't..in fact, it seemed that race relations actually got worse, not better under the Obama administration. I am not blaming the former President, but I think there is a correlation.

Politics have taken control of every element of our society, from Saturday night entertainment to Sunday afternoon football. The political parties have drawn such tight lines that no form of communication can be ignored in the larger political strategy, whether it is a morning talk show or a Hollywood awards banquet...and no other political issue is easier to cultivate than race. It is just too easy.

You criticize President Obama...you're a racist. You say you don't like rap music...you're a racist. You refer to an NBA player as a thug...you're a racist.

During the Obama years, we had several significant racial events. First was the shooting of a young black man in Ferguson, Missouri. Apparently, as the story went, a seasoned law enforcement officer stopped his cruiser in broad daylight on a sunny afternoon, then pulled out his pistol and shot six times...at a young man on his knees pleading "hands up..don't shoot!" Apparently this officer was such a racist that he just ignored the young man's pleas and pumped six shots into his chest.

This ignited a riot (of course, nothing solves a problem like a riot destroying the stores and property where the local residents live and shop) which the media reported hourly with almost gleeful enthusiasm. After that event, shootings of black suspects became a daily staple of national news. Of course, they conveniently left out a few interesting facts..such as the fact that this "child" was 18 years old, 6 feet, 4 inches tall and weighed 290 pounds , that he was stoned and that he had just robbed a convenience store two blocks away. They also seemed to ignore that a grand jury in St. Louis (with 3 black jurors) found the officer not guilty of any wrongdoing in the shooting. One has to believe that this jury saw evidence that clearly showed the officer acted appropriately and legally, but did any news organization seek to examine this additional evidence? No.

Thus began a pattern. Every night, somewhere in this nation of 230 million people, a policeman shot a black suspect without cause. Never mind that, in many of these cases, the suspect was resisting arrest or trying to flee. These kinds of details dilute the story and don't advance the agenda...which is to anger and incite the black community against law enforcement, an action which is somehow intricately linked to conservative causes and organizations, even if the officers are black.

Watching these cases on the evening news, I couldn't help but ask myself...did any Italians get man-handled by the police today? Did any Native-Americans get mistreated by cops recently? How about the Jews and Asians? I guess they all have been behaving this year.

Of course, this is ridiculous. The bottom line is that black Americans represent a potential 30 million voting block from which the Democrats have received 98% support for forty years. To maintain this, they must maintain fear and anger in this electorate and convince them that they are their savior, although there is little evidence that they have ever delivered on that promise.

I do not know what it means to be black in America today, and it would be folly for me to attempt to try to describe that reality. But I do know a few things about the race issue today...

I KNOW that there are several political organizations for which racial strife is not only advantageous but essential, the major one being the Democratic Party. If racial strife was declared dead and over tomorrow, it would leave black Americans to make their voting choices based on the same issues as everybody else...jobs and opportunity, national defense, taxes, etc. but that wouldn't work because the Democratic party cannot ever let any group start thinking about anything except their fear and hatred of Republicans.

I KNOW that encouraging black youths to disrespect the flag and anthem of their country cannot come to any good end for anyone. It teaches disrespect, anger, and it divides Americans by race, just what I thought we were trying to avoid.

I KNOW that the "gangster" model that is advanced by obscene rap music and violent movies cannot possibly help to reduce racial strife. It can only create more negative stereotypes and poor role models.

 I KNOW that gangs are destroying our black youth. I know this from personal observation, since my home town of High Point, NC is now experiencing deadly shootings on a weekly (and sometimes nightly) basis, including aimless drive-by shootings that are taking the lives of innocent children and adults while they are sitting in their homes. These gangs and their violent behavior are taking far more lives than all the racists and bad cops in this state.

I KNOW that when given a serious challenge, Americans will do almost anything to save the republic. During WWII, citizens of all walks of life joined in the effort to conserve vital materials needed for the war effort and bought war bonds to finance the war, not to mention the millions of young men and women who left their comfortable homes to sacrifice their lives and bodies to fight for the US. After the 911 attacks on our democracy. All Americans joined in prayer, then anger, then reconstruction of our pride and national strength. I sincerely believe that a serious clarion call to end racism and bigotry by a national leader who is not motivated by politics could spark a national trend to end the violence and build a peaceful, color-blind nation.

What if the national media took a break from their daily story about individual acts of racism and replaced them with stories of individual efforts end the hatred and discrimination? These stories DO exist but reporting of them does not fit the current political agenda. What if school children and young adults began to celebrate the cultural divides (as they already do) and campaign for others to follow their lead? It CAN be done. All we need is a new charismatic and dynamic leader who is not running for anything except peace and understanding to emerge from the smoke and confusion. We need a new incarnation of Martin Luther King who will speak of peace and unity as King did throughout his life. Who knows...this new messenger of hope might encourage us to stop kneeling on one knee and get back to kneeling on both!

Unfortunately, I don't see anyone (of any race or political party) seriously attempting to bring this message to the national conversation. Rather, I see just the opposite. The Democratic Party is weaponizing race relations for their own political gain and local demagogues seem to be spending as much time attacking law enforcement as they are the gangs that are clearly creating this crisis. Like most of our real challenges in this country, we are collectively too mired in political division and finger pointing to seek a real solution that doesn't affect the outcome of the next election.

One thing for sure, **I KNOW** that we can do better.

CONFESSION

I feel the constitution is the only thing saving our nation from total decline

"Congress shall pass no law" reads the opening words of the first amendment to the US Constitution. Just stop and ponder the weight of this proclamation by the statesmen who founded our nation. Their first addition to the core document was an amendment that stated what the government could NOT do!   Or consider the wording of article Ten   "The powers not delegated to the United States by the Constitution, nor prohibited by it to the states, are reserved to the states respectively, or to the people" That is the whole article! Can you imagine our present group of politicians composing such a momentous piece of legislature in such a simple and direct manner? No, neither can I. That is one of many reasons that the US Constitution must be preserved in its original form. It is the nation's roadmap and final arbiter of right and wrong by the nation's highest court. Without it, every issue would descend into a morass of political partisanship and pointless bickering.

I was handed a copy of the US Constitution at my High School Graduation, and I am referencing that very copy as I am writing this. I doubt that many high school students in the past thirty years have even seen a copy of this document, much less studied the provisions that control our government and our society. There is a reason for this omission. The US Constitution, its amendments and the Bill of Rights are an eternal thorn in the side of the Liberal aristocracy, who would like nothing more than to convince a new generation of young voters that this historical document is out of date, irrelevant in today's society, and badly in need of a modern update. God help us all if they succeed in selling that concept. After all, so much of this document is simply carved in stone. Consider the second amendment..."A well regulated militia, being necessary to the security of a free state, the right of the people to keep and bear arms, shall not be infringed."

Such straightforward and indisputable language presents a major hurdle to those that would undo the vision of our founding fathers, who were not concerned with polling data, Federal budgets, or their chances for re-election. They had escaped a tyrannous government that had ignored individual freedoms, limited citizens' rights to worship and speak freely, or protest against the state. They knew the core values that would hold together a nation dedicated to freedom and independence and, for the first time in the history of modern man, they had an opportunity to build a nation from the ground up.

Presented with a blank canvas, they knew they had but one chance to get it right.

Of course, they were just humans and were not perfect by today's historical yardstick. They were all men, all white, and many owned slaves. The fact that this was the reality of that day and time does not assuage these critics, but I would prefer to measure these historical figures by what they accomplished collectively, not what sins they committed individually. What they achieved was to compose the greatest socio-political document ever created by humankind.

But the activists on the Left are relentless in their effort to undo this contract, just as they would gladly undo every good thing President Trump has achieved in the past four years, no matter the cost. Their strategy is to just chip away at this monument to justice one piece at a time while they attempt to persuade a younger, less informed generation that this document needs to be updated and revised. For a generation who updates their computer programs every six months, this might be an easy sale. However, it would require that this generation (and others to come,) be kept in the dark as to the critical nature of this essential foundation to our democracy. This requires that constitutional education be denied or hidden from the younger generation. Today's young people are extremely intelligent and process information very fast when they have it to digest. I can only hope that they will experience the same awakening that I had as I grew a bit older and began to see the world through the eyes of a parent, taxpayer, homeowner, citizen and American.

But the critics and constitutional reformist continue to chip away, with subtle messages about the "old white men" or the "Slave Owners" or redefining the principles with phrases like "Well, the founding fathers never saw a machine gun" thus trying to open the door to re-examining the structure of the document itself. However, the founding fathers saw this debate coming too, so they structured the process to change, add or subtract from this document VERY difficult.

That is why, as conservatives (or strict constitutionalists,) we must be vigilant to keep a position where we can block any such effort even when we are in the minority, vote-wise. Today's situation in Washington is different from any other in history. The hatred of the opposition, their outrage over the current President's ability to get elected and undo much of the previous administrations legislative efforts has created an adversarial machine whose desire for retribution exceeds anything in the history of American politics. If the opposition party regains power, the tsunami of partisan legislation they will unleash will make even the most open-minded citizen gasp. The election of Donald Trump underscored the Democrats' feeble hold on the electoral process, and they will make sure next time that they cram their agenda down American's throats with a vengeance.

However, as for the constitution and its strength to hold, you must remember that one of the greatest accomplishments of the Trump administration (one which is seldom discussed,) that being his appointment of more than 180 federal judges...all for life. One more rm for the President would help ensure that this document would be reserved for at least a half century.

his is incredibly important. To ensure its longevity, The onstitution's authors placed critical limits to most of the strategies at politicians might employ to hijack the country's system of overnment and its judicial oversight. It places serious requirements n efforts to impeach a President, alter legislative checks and alances, or change voting practices. But the fact we have millions of oung voters who have never seen this historic document, much less tudied it or been informed of its importance, is troubling. As onservatives, as citizens, we MUST do a better job of educating the ounger generation about the foundations that support our overnment and society.

a new generation of lawmakers and voters ever manage to open the atcs of constitutional revision, the results will be catastrophic, egardless of which party is in charge. Just review the simple, concise nd unambiguous language our forefathers used to form this ocument. Can you imagine any of today's lawmakers in Washington ttempting to revise any portion of this historic document with the ame unselfish and bipartisan style? Impossible. Any effort to revise a ingle line in this document would inevitably disintegrate into artisan bickering, endless debate and political posturing designed to reate a policy mandate that appeases special interest groups, big onors and the Legislative majority of the day. If this revisionist ndertaking ever became a routine element of our legislative process,

I sincerely believe that it would spell the end of our Democracy as we

know it, a move that we could never undo.

We cannot allow this to happen.

CONFESSION

I am glad that Donald Trump was elected President

When I was a child, I listened as my father and the other adults discussed presidential politics. Even then, they talked about finding a candidate who was an "outsider", someone who didn't owe their candidacy to all the donors who paved their way to the White House. They prayed for a candidate that protected American interests and tried to protect American jobs in the face of foreign competition. This was long before NAFTA and the era of globalization but I assure you, in a nation that has lost millions of jobs to overseas manufacturers, that this sentiment has not waned. Nor has the conviction that immigrants should become citizens and adapt to the American culture. This does not represent any "hatred" by the American citizens, rather it simply demonstrates the obvious...that they and their ancestors made that transition and they feel it is a logical and patriotic requirement.

Donald Trump ran on promises that resonated with the American people, then he proceeded to fulfill these commitments, even without the support of his own party. Since he has taken office, he has accomplished more in almost four years than any president in my lifetime, although you wouldn't know it by watching the evening news. We are enjoying the most robust economy in 60 years with the lowest unemployment possible. Businesses, large and small, are flourishing and companies are hiring people by the thousands.

Some pundits debate why Trump won the election. This baffles me. He simply told the American people what they wanted to hear, then delivered. The politicos call this "populism" as if that is a bad thing. I call it common sense. From where I stand, you are either a populist or a globalist, and I am pretty sure the American people prefer the former. He has exposed the hypocrisy of the left repeatedly. After all, how could the (so-called) party of the people try to derail an administration that has put millions to work and taken hundreds of thousands off welfare roles?

Donald Trump is not a classic statesman. He is eccentric, crude, bombastic and confrontational. He doesn't take crap from anyone without throwing it back and that is just one of the many attributes that millions of Americans love about him. He has ignored all the rules that govern Washington politics and it has been hilarious to observe. He has totally upset the Washington applecart for the entire political establishment (on both sides of the aisle) and it has infuriated the powers-to-be like nothing in the history of our government. Prior to

Trump, politicians showed up in the halls of power, gave a few speeches for the TV cameras, voted as they had promised the night before in private caucuses, then headed down the street for dinner with the loyal opposition before stopping by the Ambassador's house for drinks. Everything was scripted and everyone respected the opposition's turf. Big donors were given the subsidy they lobbied for and their family members enjoyed puff jobs at some foreign embassy. Every four or eight years, the reigning party let the other take the ball with a chest-thumping outcry but without too much personal animosity, lest they lose their committee chair or their invitation to the annual Christmas banquet. It was a "Good ol' boys" system that had worked effectively for decades. The new President, Congressman, or Senator arrived in town, met the powers that be, learned the rules, then settled into a comfortable and privileged life of statesmanship.

At least that is the way I see it, or have observed it for fifty years. Every conservative candidate in my lifetime has promised to reverse this system or even to "Reduce the size of government." Finally, it occurred to me, a politician promising to shrink the US government is like a candidate running for President of the Plumbers Union promising to shrink the membership of Plumbers. Then came Trump. A bombastic, confident businessman who knew how to get things done, a man who owed nothing to anyone in Washington, a candidate who promised to "Drain the Swamp" and change the system. Except this guy meant it, and that must have sent shivers through the Washington establishment. They were accustomed to candidates making these kinds of commitments but the idea that someone would actually do it terrified them. After all, this just isn't done. But this guy was serious and for God's sake, he had his own plane!

From the beginning, the media and the political pundits described him as an "idiot" but, behind closed doors, they must have known better. A total novice to the national political process, this genuine outsider ran a masterful campaign, campaigning at a pace no mortal could keep up with...least of all, Hillary Clinton. He hit the right states at the right time, ignoring the critics, polls and never apologizing to anyone for anything. The voters identified with him and were energized for one very simple reason...they recognized that this candidate was different, that he might just deliver on his promises, something no one had seen in their voting lifetimes. Then, against all odds, he won.

Taking office, he maintained the same decisive, unstoppable determination that got him there, ignoring critics and naysayers from the media and his own party, He plowed forward in the face of opposition that would have destroyed a weaker individual, ignoring critics, pundits and weak members of his own party while accomplishing more in three and a half years than any President in my lifetime...

* Strongest economy in 60 years with companies, large and small, thriving.

* Lowest unemployment in fifty years with more American working than at any time in history.

4 million new jobs have been created since he took office.

Jobless claims lowest in five decades.

Renegotiating unfair trade agreements that will benefit American industry for years to come.

Longest bull market in the history of Wall Street.

Raising oil production to surpass Russia and Saudi Arabia, making the US the world's largest producer of crude oil and making the US energy independent for the first time in recent memory.

Moving the US Embassy to Jerusalem, a promise made by every President in the past four decades.

Ending the Iran Nuclear deal, possibly the most important move of his Presidency.

Renegotiating NAFTA. The new USMCA will improve trade equity and reduce China's unfair advantage on trade.

Taking a stand on illegal immigration.

The list of Trump's accomplishments would fill a book, but a list of those achievements that have been publicized by the news media wouldn't fill a post-it note. Therefore, voters contemplating their choice for President in 2020 are working without critical information. All they have seen on the news for almost four years is one

investigation after another, and a never-ending line of talking head
spouting how Trump is "A Threat to Democracy" and why removin
him from office is a matter of life and death. From where I stand, th
lives of Americans are immeasurably better than they were just fou
years ago. I see "Help Wanted" signs everywhere I go. New companie
are opening daily and people are being hired by the hundreds. As fo
our international standing, I view an international community tha
sees a strong, no-nonsense leader who means business and doesn
take "no" for an answer. Nowhere do I see any threat to my life o
safety due to this President's actions or rhetoric.

The only "Threat to Democracy" I observe is a democratic party and
national media that refuses to accept the results of the last nationa
election, a group willing to ignore the obvious achievements of thi
administration and are willing to do "anything" to reverse the wishe
of 63 million voters simply because the result didn't suit them. I can
help wondering...what if they succeed? Have they considered the long
term damage they have done to our electoral process? Do they no
realize they are establishing a dangerous precedent? Shall the tw
parties slug out every administrative term with such useless and sel
serving conflicts?

Of course, I know the answer. The current mainstream media think
that these tactics will only ever surface again against a conservativ
candidate since they control 90% of the information flow. They plan t
help place a suitable Liberal Democrat in the office, then watch a
everything returns to the status quo. However, I believe that if thes

obviously biased attacks succeed in removing or defeating Donald Trump, the result this time will be markedly different. For one, Donald Trump will not go quietly into the night. Secondly, his followers will not take lightly this insult to their voting privileges. Faced with candidates that are openly socialist, who state unequivocally that they wish to confiscate firearms from private citizens, individuals that make it clear that they plan to "undo" the accomplishments of the Trump administration, I think the blow-back will be as historic and unprecedented as the bizarre campaign to destroy the Trump presidency.

But Trump seems oblivious to these attacks and seems to enjoy tweaking these adversaries. They hate his late night "tweets" but like everything else about Trump, this issue has its humorous flip side. First, you have the Democratic Party, who thought they owned the concept of social media, unlike those stodgy old Republicans. Then Trump turned it inside out without a blink, leaving the media to simply "Retweet" his nightly emissions to show how unhinged he was. But for me, his use of social media as a media weapon was the ultimate act of defiance. For my entire adult life, I watched as Republican Presidents would give a two hour speech in Des Moines, after which the New York media would reduce it to one awkward line, one mispronounced word, one inaccurate statistic. Now, for the first time in political history, a conservative leader could punch out a message to 50 million citizens without any media filter, an act that clearly infuriated the mainstream news organizations, which were reduced to reporting his latest tweets again on the evening news. What a revelation!

I supported both Bush Presidents, but it became infuriating to watch how they would take the opposition slings and arrows without even trying to fight back. It had to give any observer the feeling that they were part of the Washington Establishment, someone who didn't want to ruffle too many feathers along the way. Trump LOVES to ruffle feathers and to watch him do so has been the best political show I have ever seen. His sheer ambivalence to opposition reminds me of a heavyweight fighter at weigh-in...staring straight at his opponent without fear or hesitation. His confidence in the face of overwhelming opposition should be an inspiration to anyone fighting their way through this world, and it is clear that he has everyone in Washington totally befuddled.

I feel it is essential that we elect Trump for another four years for two reasons. The first is that I am convinced that we will never see another one like him, and if he accomplished half of what he accomplished in the first term, he will advance the cause of democracy and conservatism so far, it will take the Democratic Party twenty years to recover. The second is that he is just so damn entertaining!

To appreciate my support of this President requires a fundamental understanding of what I expect from this leader of the free world. For me, the idea that the President of the United States holds and maintains the nation's moral compass is no longer viable. For me, that ship sailed with Bill Clinton. I consider the President to be the CEO of the nation whose major responsibilities are as follows...

1. PROTECT AND MAINTAIN THE ECONOMY. Support the nation's industries and small businesses, create and protect jobs for everyone who wants to work.

2. MAINTAIN OUR NATIONAL DEFENSE. Protect our borders, strengthen our military and keep our enemies at bay.

3. ABIDE BY THE CONSTRAINTS OF THE CONSTITUTION. I believe this is essential and that any other path is folly. When in doubt...follow the plan.

As I prepare this book for publication, the congress is conducting "Impeachment" hearings, attempting to take a phone call the President of the United States made to a third world potentate, and turn it into crime deserving of his removal from office. The basis for this undertaking is so flimsy, it would be comical if it weren't being conducted by the legislative body of the most powerful nation on earth. Everyone in this legislative body knows this proceeding is a sham, a cheap parlor trick designed to accomplish but one goal...to convince uninformed voters that this President is so horrible, so corrupt, so evil that we must remove him from office. Of course, even those conducting the "hearings" know that will not happen, since Republicans control the Senate, which must approve the removal effort.

So why are they conducting this mock trial? The answer is simple and everyone in Washington knows it. They are doing this for the same reason they conducted the Kavanaugh embarrassment, the same reason as the Mueller hearings. It is all part of the Democratic Party's 2020 campaign to defeat Trump in the next election by alarming enough voters to sway the numbers in their favor in November. Of course, these hearing will go nowhere but there will be a next act. After this sham is complete, they will go for Trump's income taxes, then drag up some beauty queens that say he groped them 20 years ago. There will be no end until November. Then, if by some miracle, he survives and triumphs in November 2020, there will be new accusations of "Russian Collusion", etc. etc. etc.

No matter what your party affiliation is, I have to challenge you to answer two questions? One...what has the Democratic Party accomplished in the past four years? Two...if the Liberal Democratic platform is so superior to all others, why can't they simply present their programs, values and platform to the American people, then let the voters decide? If Donald Trump is such a dangerous and ineffective leader, why wouldn't the American people look at his record from the past four years, then vote for the opposing candidate?

The answer is simple. The Democratic Party has no candidate with even the slightest chance to win in November 2020 without either removing Trump from office or damaging his reputation to the point that voters either refrain from voting or throw their vote away. The idea that a majority of American voters will support a candidate that is openly socialist, that promises to disarm citizens and raise taxes to und bizarre, other-worldly social programs that will cost trillions of dollars is just not realistic unless they don't know what they are voting for, or unless they are just voting AGAINST Trump. That latter is the Democratic Party's greatest hope.

This is no way to run a democracy.

CONFESSION

I think the majority of Americans are conservative at their core

Proving this hypothesis could be problematic. One could conduct poll, but as I have stated earlier, this process has been so bastardize that I no longer feel it is a viable means to measure public opinior One could take a more abstract approach to the question, measurin other benchmarks, such as subscribers of newsworthy media outlets.

The success and dominance of Fox News, who has ranked No. 1 i cable news for fifteen years in a row.

Or Rush Limbaugh's radio audience of nearly twenty million, th largest radio audience of its kind for twenty-seven years.

Or just review the list of top radio hosts in America, which is dominated by conservative names such as Sean Hannity and Laura Ingraham.

Before I continue, it is interesting to note that liberals cling to the idea that conservatives have hijacked "talk radio" (isn't NPR talk radio?) and thus excluded liberal voices. I know for a fact that this isn't true. When Rush Limbaugh first appeared on the airwaves, a number of national liberal talk shows were launched (remember Air America?) and virtually all of them failed. My observation on this is that whenever major liberal voices speak, they make certain they are preaching to the choir. Watch any rally by a major liberal voice, and you will see an audience filled with members of the NAACP, NOW, IBEW, NEA, and GLAAD. They transport them in by buses with prefab protest signs and a script as to when to chant and cheer. Try to put these same orators on the public airwaves where they have to talk to real people and answer real questions, and they fold up like a cheap tent. Imagine being on the air in Alabama and trying to defend full term abortion or giving $150 billion to Iran? Good luck.

However, I think the best way to try to comprehend the true heart of actual Americans and why conservatism survives is to take a step back and view the landscape as a fictional country. Try to imagine a country with three hundred thirty million people who are represented by two major political factions, both of which seem equally divided. Now consider that one party controls virtually all of the news media, every actor, every movie producer, every musician and rock star, all TV production from morning talk shows to afternoon show hosts, every documentary filmmaker, every college professor and scientist, every newspaper editor and reporter. What political party would you think was dominant in that country's government? And if you found that the opposition party was consistently winning at state, local, and national levels, what would you conclude?

That is actually where we are, and the Democratic Party knows it. Otherwise, they would just simply present their platforms and philosophies to voters, then let them decide. But they can't afford to do that because it just wouldn't play in Peoria. That is why the Dems are working full-time, twenty-four hours a day trying to destroy Donald Trump because they know they cannot defeat him at the polls. For the past six months, they have been working to find a presidential candidate to challenge him at the polls, and they have yet to find a single one who could get elected dog catcher.

However, fundamental differences between liberals and conservatives make it difficult to identify them as a species. Currently, liberal activists are the most vocal, violent, and aggressive in political history. Meanwhile, the typical conservative voter tends to shy away from these organized conflicts and protests, preferring to express their views at the ballot box. This dichotomy makes it difficult to read the actual views of the populace, by anyone who is attempting to get an accurate reading. I know this from personal observation. I know scores of conservative voters who have told me personally that they will not put a Trump bumper sticker on their car for fear of vandalism or personal attacks. These same people tend to hang up on telephone pollsters and avoid online bickering. I can't help but recall the label "Silent Majority," a term I think may apply more accurately now than when it first emerged twenty years ago.

Not that the media pollsters care anyway. Their plan is to repeatedly report "polling data" that indicate that the majority of Americans hate Trump and support his removal from office, with the assumption that there will always be a number of under-informed voters who look at the daily news reports and assume that the president is a horrible traitor who is on the brink of political destruction. This plan is not without value, especially as it applies to the "independent" voters, a category that is a polite way to describe people who simply do not understand the American political process and think that listening to the daily news reports will help them reach a fair and logical choice. Trust me, politicians on both sides salivate when they examine this confused but well-meaning group of idealists.

One characteristic is shared by a great many Democratic, Republican, and independent voters. They love the country and want to do the right thing when they vote and choose a candidate. Most of these people are not political "wonks" who study every issue and drill down to see the actual political motivations and goals behind every issue. They don't have time and dislike politics anyway. Therefore, all they can do is listen to the evening news and read the headlines, then throw the dice. This is what the Democratic Party (and the media they control) is counting on. Since the current president took office, an independent watchdog group estimates that ninety-four percent of all news coverage has been critical of Trump, which also means they have consistently ignored and suppressed the facts about the incredible economy this country is enjoying and the monumental strides this president has made to regain fair and balanced trade agreements that will affect our nation's economy for decades.

By now, you may have concluded that my top concern is the economic status of the country, and you would be right. I have seen the country when the economy is strong and when it is weak. Trust me, when the economy is strong and people are working, all the other problems we talk about (poverty, opportunity, unemployment, equality, hunger, and housing) begin to work themselves out. Do we have other issues that are important to our citizens? Yes, but nothing can be done about any of these challenges if people are not working. It is the foundation on which all progress must be built. If you doubt this, think about the challenges you and your family face every day (paying the bills, financing your kids braces, saving for college) then imagine you or your spouse loses their job. What is your priority now? Getting a job becomes job number one and everything else hinges on that, right? The country is no different...full employment eliminates need for food stamps, unemployment checks, housing subsidies, health care...everything that a paycheck should cover. Simplistic? Perhaps, but I assure you that nothing solves more problems than a JOB. Several million jobs will solve several million problems.

et, the Democratic Party has made a living for fifty years building rograms for people who don't have jobs. On the surface, that sounds dmirable, but you have to ask yourself, what situation benefits this arty more ...poverty or prosperity? And why are they so determined ɔ end this historic economic boon and pray (openly) for a recession?

hink about it...HARD.

CONFESSION

I Consider Media Bias Against the South the Ultimate Insult

I love New York City. I consider it the greatest city on the planet. Ove
the years, I have walked the streets of New York from the Battery t
Central Park. I have savored the city's incredible restaurants, deli
museums, parks, people, music, and landmarks. I have enjoyed thi
metropolis in all kinds of weather, from searing heat to blinding snov
It is beautiful no matter what the season.

I also love movies...all kinds of movies, from black & white classics t
modern day comedies and dramas. I especially love movies set in Ne\
York, and I can't view a movie released before 2000 without lookin
for the Twin Towers, a habit I'll wager is shared by almost every movi
fan. I have enjoyed movies set in this city in every season of the yea

from "Miracle on 34th Street" and "Elf" to "The Odd Couple," "Barefoot In The Park," and "Sleepless in Seattle."

Likewise, I have spent a considerable amount of time in the Deep South, especially since I married a beautiful young girl from Birmingham, Alabama. And just as I appreciate stories featuring New York City, I love to watch movies set in the South from Mississippi to South Carolina. However, I have noticed an undeniable trend in the filming of movies set in this region. It is always summertime, blistering hot, with magnolia trees weeping in the yard as an old white man sits on the porch of an antebellum mansion, fanning himself and sipping a mint julep while underlings (usually black) stand in the yard looking up at him as they beseech him for some favor. After forty years of movie viewing, I have NEVER seen a movie set in Alabama while the weather was cold or snowing. I find that odd, since after living in the South for forty years, I can attest that it gets cold in Mississippi, snows in Alabama, and freezes in Georgia. I can only conclude that the writers or producers of these films have never been in the South during the winter or that they simply don't think that such a scene fits the script and story. I am fairly sure it is the latter.

For instance, ten minutes into the opening of the thriller "Kiss the Girls" the camera pans over miles of dense forest before descending into the city of Durham, North Carolina. Shortly thereafter, Dr. Alex Cross (Morgan Freeman) enters the office of the Durham police, where he is left cooling his heels all afternoon until he pushes his way into the office of the police chief, who is named HATFIELD. The racist message here is anything but subtle.

To attest to the entertainment industry's concept of the South, you need only review the history of television's schedules since the invention of the medium. Virtually all programming set in the Southern environment portrays an ignorant, country individual or family struggling to survive with life, if not the English language. This was true from the beginning with shows like "The Real McCoys," "The Beverly Hillbillies," "Green Acres," "The Andy Griffith Show," "The Dukes of Hazzard," "Hee Haw," "Gomer Pyle: USMC," and countless others. Meanwhile, serious dramas (where actors use multisyllabic words and possess all their teeth) are set in New York, Chicago, Los Angeles, or any major metropolitan area north of the Mason-Dixon Line, from TV shows like "Law and Order," "Hill Street Blues," "LA Law," and "Boston Legal" to "Frazier," "Cheers," "Blue Bloods," "Bull," "FBI," and "Madame Secretary."

The message is clear. Obviously, the Northern states and the West Coast are populated by intelligent, well-educated citizens who perform important jobs and accomplish great things that make the world a better place. Meanwhile, the South is clearly overrun with toothless, ignorant, gun-toting racists who live in shacks, drive pickup trucks with gun racks, wave the Confederate Flag, hate everyone of color, and are praying for an opportunity to renew the Civil War. Like all social templates used by the media, this image is critical to the long-term liberal agenda, since the South consistently votes conservative and elects Republicans. Obviously, these people must be demonized and neutralized. The fact that this image is totally inaccurate is irrelevant to the media and the political party they represent. All opposition must be destroyed at any cost. Facts seldom get in the way of a good story about the Old South, but I would like to try to offer a few items for you to consider...

* California has more registered gun owners than Alabama, North Carolina, South Carolina or Georgia.

* New York issued more hunting licenses in 2019 than Alabama.

* There are more colleges and universities in Georgia (210) than Connecticut, Maine, Rhode Island, Vermont, Washington, Wisconsin, New Hampshire, Maryland, or Oregon.

* The busiest airport in the world is located in Atlanta, Georgia.

* Virtually all Southern states are gaining population while most of the North shrinks.

This last item should befuddle even the most devout liberal. After all, if the South is a haven for ignorant, uneducated racists, why are lifelong Democrats moving there in droves? Either this part of the nation has been grossly mischaracterized or a lifetime of astronomical taxes and liberal politics has led some intrepid Yankees to explore this dark, dangerous region. I am certain the former is true, but the latter seems just as likely.

But the arrival of Northern Democrats to the New South has some puzzling elements for this conservative. After settling in a beautiful, warm, and thriving Southern state where their tax bill and real estate budget has been reduced by as much as eighty percent, one would think that their politics would soon reflect a change in philosophy, but as yet, this transition has not evolved. They cling to their party affiliation like graduates cling to their alma mater. Thus many states, including North Carolina, are now colorfully designated as "purple" to describe a political mix in a state that was always considered a "red" state. I can only attribute this continued allegiance to tribal loyalty or to a fundamental misunderstanding of what forces financed their escape from the socialist Shangri La where they have spent most of their lifetimes but now want to escape.

The sad fact is most people simply don't spend that much time studying how political forces affect their lives. They hear their friends say, "We hate Trump," and they join the jeering crowd. Someone tells a conservative that all Democrats are socialists, and they take to Facebook to attack friends they have known for decades. Both groups are simply "reacting" to partisan rhetoric instead of thinking things through by research and rational thought. Neither party wants you to do much thinking or analysis...They simply want you to react and pull the lever for their tribe.

Personally, I can attest to one undeniable fact...Southerners are not a bunch of racist yahoos riding around in pickup trucks burning crosses and waving Confederate flags. Nor are most Democrats socialist emagogues who want to destroy our country and denounce our flag. Today's political landscape is dominated by extreme points of view, and it is essential that every voter to push through the fog, open their minds to points of view, and try to examine the FACTS before joining the mob.

In North Carolina, we welcome the unbridled "immigration" of Northerners to our beautiful, scenic, and conservative homeland. But I for one, would only plead that they look upon our state as more than just a great place to retire, but as a great example of how a Southern state can be friendly, inclusive, tolerant, and fiscally sound without oppressive taxation or regulation. Just face it, you live here now, which makes you Southerners.

Welcome y'all. And bless your little heart!

CONFESSION

I Have Some Valuable Advice for the Democratic Party

If the Democratic leadership wishes to ever win a national election by selling their political ideas rather than just demonizing the opposing party, I would recommend they consider doing the following...

BUY A CALENDAR. You will notice almost immediately that it is not 1968. Marching down the streets with signs that are screen printed to look home-made while chanting catchy slogans simply won't work for the typical citizen today. Americans are working in record numbers, and they are puzzled by where all these protesters work and why they get so many days off.

DITCH THE POLLS. I know you believe that you need only convince voters that everyone else believes your findings except them, but there is a problem. Your polls have been wrong so many times that most voters no longer place any value in them. Plus, believe it or not, most Americans know what a *"push"* poll is and what *"sampling"* means. They simply are no longer falling for it.

HIDE YOUR AGENDA. I thought you knew this one. The only way to sell your socialist, globalist, and apologist platform is to conceal it until after the election. How could you forget this cardinal rule? You must be slipping. I suggest rebranding the socialist agenda with something catchy and confusing.

STOP CALLING PEOPLE NAMES. I realize that you think all conservative voters are ignorant, uneducated, and toothless Walmart shoppers, but you seem to forget...Walmart has a LOT of shoppers. Further, until you manage to repeal the Constitution, every poor, ignorant, deplorable citizen still gets a vote...and somehow, even the most uneducated, tobacco-spitting voter seems to know how to get to the polls without much assistance. Branding them all as racist, homophobic deplorables is not a winning strategy.

SEND HILLARY ON VACATION. Perhaps Bora Bora. I realize that you consider her to be your standard bearer, but I believe you have overestimated her popularity even within your party. They voted for her because she was the candidate. When she is not on the ticket, she is just another whining loser whose very voice causes millions of voters to grind their teeth.

FIND SOME MESSAGE OTHER THAN "FREE." Free is considered the most magical term in product advertising, but there is one big problem for you as long as a conservative economy is rolling. People with jobs don't need welfare, free health care, guaranteed salaries, or free oil-changes for life. Maybe you need to talk about what you would do for the country and its citizens if they were not poor, unemployed, and hungry.

WAVE THE FLAG. I know you hate this fascist symbol, but millions of Americans out in the hinterland still love their country and salute this symbol of freedom and national pride. Just putting one up behind a candidate at rallies is not enough. Put a flag decal on your campaign bus, sneak a flag pin into your lapel when in Alabama. You know…optics! (Just till after the election.)

TALK TO SOME REAL AMERICANS. Go down to Alabama, or South Carolina, or almost anywhere but Washington, D.C., New York, or California. Visit some diners, bars, churches, and beauty shops (you might want to avoid VFWs) and ask them questions like *"How do you feel about giving Iran $150 billion dollars to build a nuclear program?"* or *"Do you support the concept of full term abortion even on the delivery table?"* The experience will be an eye-opening, to say the least.

AVOID DETAILS WHEN EXPLAINING YOUR PLATFORM. If you start trying to explain how to pay for free college, forgiveness of all student debt, free health care and guaranteed salaries for all, you will just get stuck in the weeds. Keep it simple.

PRAY FOR A RECESSION. Nothing could help your cause like millions of Americans losing their jobs and homes. Then your *"welfare for all"* programs will start to make sense.

It is important to clarify, at this point, that these admonitions are aimed at the leadership of the Democratic Party, not specifically at individual liberal voters. I include this notation because I am convinced that the vast majority of Democratic voters do not fully understand what their own party really stands for. They seem convinced that their party represents the poor and downtrodden, protects their tribe (whatever minority they fit into) while those mean old Republicans are planning their next Klan rally. When I engage them politely on the larger issues, they seem clueless and indignant about the existence of a greater global strategy to undermine the strength of this country and the institutions that support it. They watch the news breathlessly and hang on every word from their journalistic standard bearer, who is ALWAYS reporting the *"victim of the day,"* including why the Republican Party is responsible for their misery. One piece of advice that the Democratic Party does not need is this…

Keep the base energized and angry.

If you are a loyal long-time Democrat, I would like you to ponder this question. Are you a loyal party member because you honestly believe in and support the party's current platform, or are you just a longtime team player who can't imagine changing sides? Or have your party's voices convinced you that the opposition is so evil and dastardly that your support of them would end the world as we know it?

No doubt you dislike Donald Trump, his voice, his mannerisms, the very sound of his voice, but try to put all this anger aside for a moment, then take an honest assessment of the last four years. Have you looked at the economy? Do you see the thousands of people who are working at jobs that didn't even exist four years ago? Are YOU better off financially now than you were four years ago? Would you support the defeat of Donald Trump even if it meant millions of workers lost their jobs, an increase in your taxes, and a long-term drop in the stock market and YOUR investments? These are the questions you MUST answer before you vote in November.

But your party doesn't want you to think about these issues. That is why they work seven days a week creating dramas designed to convince you that another four years of Trump will be catastrophic, while almost NEVER mentioning the current U.S. economy. If these predictions concern you, take a close look at the past four years. Did the world end under Donald Trump? Did we start any wars? Have we experienced any serious attacks of terrorism on U.S. soil? Have any countries seriously threatened to attack the United States? Has it

ccurred to you that a strong, aggressive, no-nonsense leader may be
ust what the United States needs at this point in history?

o you don't like Donald Trump? No problem. You're not voting for a
ew son-in-law or the president of your neighborhood watch. You are
oting for the leader of the free world, the CEO of your nation, the
ecision maker who rules your nation's economy. You can choose a
veak-kneed socialist or a strong leader who puts YOUR nation first.

ick one and live with it.

CONFESSION

I Have Some Advice For Young Americans

I hope this collection of essays makes its way to some of the millions of young people preparing to take over the country's workforce, businesses, home schools, and ballot boxes. If I had the chance, I would welcome the opportunity to share the following thoughts with each one of you...

1. **DON'T BELIEVE EVERYTHING YOU HEAR** or read! The world is full of forces that wish to hijack your brain and your vote. Some of your decisions will stay with you for a lifetime, and a wrong decision may come back to haunt you (See Chapter 2). The world is in your hands...don't blow it!

2. **RESPECT YOUR ELDERS.** I know they seem old-fashioned and out of touch. I realize you think they are unfamiliar with your world.

and the issues that are paramount to you and your generation. But they possess one thing you do not, decades of first-hand experience with how the world works and why bad decisions can change a life. Their successes AND failures can teach you valuable lessons. Their stories are true, and they want the best for you, no strings attached.

3. **DO YOUR OWN RESEARCH.** Watch, listen, and read everything on a subject before you draw a critical decision. Most information sources (newscasters, professors, celebrities) have a view skewed by highly partisan personal agendas, whether they are liberal or conservative.

4. **OBTAIN A COPY OF THE U.S. CONSTITUTION.** This may sound boring or even pointless, but this document is the operating manual for this country and every freedom you enjoy. Your very ability to read this book depends on that document, and any changes to it would have an immediate and irreversible effect on your life.

5. **LISTEN TO MANY VOICES.** before you make an important decision. I'm sure you followed this policy before choosing a school, career, car, or even friends. But when it comes to social issues or the environment, too many of your friends are simply following the crowd and adopting positions that they have not personally investigated. This is called "Group Think." Don't just follow...lead.

6. **LEARN HOW POLITICS REALLY WORK.** You may be saying, "I'm not interested in politics." Unfortunately, you don't really have that choice, unless you want the world around you to change irrevocably without your input. Politics affects EVERYTHING in your daily life, from what you eat to what you drive, even what you can say! The secret is to understand not just what the voices are saying but WHY they are saying it. Everyone has an agenda...You need to know what that is.

7. **TAKE CARE OF THE PLANET.** Help initiate conservation efforts (as I'm sure you already do) and reduce pollution, BUT make certain that major, politically motivated global initiatives do not hamstring the U.S. economy or weaken our worldwide competitive position. This may sound like a political compromise, but you must always remember...our country's economic strength is paramount because it creates and maintains JOBS. Without jobs, people can't eat. When people can't feed themselves and their families, all other concerns become irrelevant. Trust me, you don't want to see that happen...it is a situation our nation has seen, and one that we never want to see again.

8. **LEARN TO LOVE YOUR COUNTRY.** You often hear the slogan "Take care of your planet, it is the only one you have." That is absolutely true, but it is equally true about your country. For some reason that I find incomprehensible, some very powerful political forces and voices have made it clear that they are ashamed of what I consider the greatest nation on earth. If it isn't, why are so many people from all over this planet fighting to get here? You have lived

your life, up till now, in a time of peace and historic prosperity. But this environment didn't happen by accident and could change overnight if the wrong people take charge of it. Millions of Americans have suffered and died to protect this nation. All you have to do in stand up, put your hand over your heart, and sing!

9. **LEARN WHAT SOCIALISM REALLY MEANS.** Like most liberal programs, this one sounds great. We all throw into a collective pile, let the government provide everything from health care to housing, college education, and guaranteed salaries. However, before you sign on to this governmental nirvana, you must understand several key elements of this initiative. This first is that it will cost an enormous amount of money, which can only be funded by taxes. Do you know how much money the U.S. government collects each year? Like you or me , the United States has an income. It is approximately $4 trillion. Every analysis of the programs presented by the current Democratic candidates indicates that it would take at least $30 trillion to finance, which means that you would have to give up eighty percent (at least) of your income to pay for what you are going to get for free. If you doubt that, simply look at any nation that is operating on a socialistic basis. They all collect an enormous amount of each citizen's paycheck before they dole it back out, at their discretion, to the populace.

Further, you must understand that socialism is not just an alternative economic system. It is alternate political system. To fully institute a socialistic program in the United States, you would have to essentially replace capitalism and democracy. After all, what would happen after the socialistic system was in place, then the voters decided to repeal it? That just wouldn't work. Socialism requires an "all or nothing" commitment with no turning back. Are you ready for that?

10. **LEARN TO ASK QUESTIONS.** If someone says "All college will be free," you might want to ask "What if one college is 40k a year, but another is 25k?" If they say, "We will forgive all college loans," you might inquire "What about the graduates who have already paid their loans, do they get a rebate?" if you hear that the oceans will rise ten feet in the next twenty years, you might want to find out "How much have they risen in the past twenty?" People of all stripes who would try to convince you of anything tend to hate people who ask questions. That is why attendees to political "town halls" are always pre-selected with approved questions and canned answers. No matter whose story you are hearing, it always pays to question their facts and opinions. Trust me, they are counting on people to just take their story at face value. It pays to ask questions.

I could go on, but you get the idea. This is your life, your brain, and your decisions. Don't let anybody hijack it without your permission. Never mind what your friends think. Make your own choices. One more word of advice...in ten years, half of these people won't be your friends!

ne more word of advice. If you are actively anticipating the upcoming 020 elections, you have no doubt been convinced that removing resident Trump from office will save the planet, eliminate all rejudice and bigotry, and make the country a kinder, gentler nation, while punishing billionaires for their wealth and defeating those mean ld Republicans. Unfortunately, the pundits and prophets delivering hese lofty promises have left out a few critical facts about that otential transfer of power and how it will affect YOU and your life lmost immediately. Without a doubt, the election of any of the emocratic candidates competing for the office of president at the ime of this book's publication will undoubtedly result in the ollowing...

* **SUBSTANTIAL INCREASES IN INTEREST RATES** for everything from your car, home or college loans.

* **DRASTIC INCREASES IN INCOME TAXES**. If your government hopes to spend $30 trillion on social give-aways, it has to be paid for, one way or another.

* **HIGHER PRICES FOR GASOLINE AND ON ALL KINDS OF FUEL**. All the candidates are anti-oil and anti-coal. You can't deliver on their draconian campaign promises without punishing both.

* **RETURN OF TRADE IMBALANCES WITH CHINA AND OTHERS**. This may mean nothing to you now, but it will affect the prices of everything you buy, your income, and your overall prosperity.

* **RISING UNEMPLOYMENT AND WEAKER JOB MARKET.** If all c
  the above predictions are correct (and they are), the job forecas
  can't go anywhere but down. Jobs will become harder to find, an
  incentives for new hires will shrink, as will bonuses and raises.

* **LOWER STOCK PRICES AND A STOCK MARKET DOWNTURN**
  This includes your 401K, your stock options, your stock portfolio
  and retirement plans (ditto for your parent's investments).

How, you are probably asking, can this unknown private citizens mak
such bold predictions without a degree in economics of high finance?
can only reply that there are all kinds of education to be had in thi
world, and one that includes six decades of business ownership
investment, success and failure, and political observation empower
one with a unique ability to see the difference between th
prospective arrival of good times or bad.

Granted, this kind of economic forecasting traditionally would requir
the experience and education far exceeding mine. However, even
glance at the campaign platforms of the 2020 Democratic candidate
renders this argument moot. These far left socialists are proposing th
most radical social programs in the history of this nation. Thes
initiatives would cost an astronomical amount, and their othe
promises (elimination of internal combustion engines and oil, fre
health care for all, etc.) would cripple our economy and impact ever
citizen's life and their plans for the future, especially YOU. As
yourself, as you listened to these candidates to run the most powerfu

and successful nation on earth...how many even mentioned their plan to maintain this current economic boom? Think about it. Do they promise a strong economy or just a welfare state for everyone when this one collapses? One thing is certain, if their radical agenda is enacted (with your support) we are all going to NEED these programs to survive.

Our nation's future is literally in your hands. Please don't blow it.

CONFESSION

I Think I Can Help Voters Make Their Decision in the Next Presidential Election.

At this writing, the citizens of the United States are facing a decision that will affect the rest of their lifetimes. With all the nonsense and distractions created by the left and their friends in the media, it may be confusing for many voters to reach a decision on who should lead the nation. After all, the current president has been investigated, criticized, impeached, and accused of everything from fraud to treason. It would be easy to forget what issues will be decided by the outcome of the next election. So I have developed a simple questionnaire that I think may help you see through the current political haze and find a reason to vote for the candidate who will decide your fate for the next four years. It is simple...just answer YES or NO.

1. Do you think giving Iran $150 billion dollars to build a nuclear program was a good idea?

2. Would you support the idea of totally open borders with no requirements for ID, passports, or visas?

3. Would you support a total revision of the U.S. Constitution?

4. Would you prefer the elimination of state's rights?

5. Would you support removing Trump even if it meant losing millions of US jobs?

6. Do you think Justice Kavanaugh received a fair hearing?

7. Would you prefer socialism to our present form of government?

8. Would you prefer a national "free" health care system?

9. Do you find the U.S. flag or national anthem offensive?

10. Do you support full term abortion up to and including the point of birth?

If you answered "YES" to more than five questions, you definitely need to pull the lever for the Democratic Party every chance you get. If you answered most of your questions with "NO," then you should ignore the worrisome news reports and vote Republican at the polls. You may be puzzled by some of the questions since they don't seem to match up to the issues of the day, but that is really the point of this exercise. You have to understand the long-term agenda for the party you support before you vote. The issues you see blasted on the news twenty-four hours a day are just smoke-screens designed to distract you from seeing the big picture. The real choice is between a party that believes that government is the answer to every problem and that it is the responsibility of that party to decide what you eat, smoke, drive, and read. They believe you are incapable of making these decisions on your own. This group equates equality with sameness. They wish to destroy gender identities so everyone looks and acts the same, even to the point of criminalizing the terms "he, she, her, and him." They believe the U.S. Constitution is an outdated document that should be torn up or renegotiated to suit their agenda. They want to remove your right to bear arms and protect yourself from criminals or a criminal government. They want to replace our capitalist democracy with socialism, a form of government that has failed everywhere it has been tried. They believe that individual rights should be second to the power and wisdom of the state. They believe that people are fundamentally weak and need the government to exist and survive. They aspire to a "global" society where there is no United States, just individual nation states in an international socialist wheel.

The other option is the party that believes in true "freedom." That includes the freedom to choose your doctor, your food, your car, your lifestyle, your religion, and your opinion. This party believes in a strong military, national defense, fair trade, secure borders, and the strict interpretation of the Constitution. They do not believe that the nation's citizens are weak and helpless, or in need of constant help rom the government. They are optimistic about the nation's future, about your future, about your children's future. They do not believe that the world is collapsing. They believe that every problem has a solution. They believe that a strong economy is the foundation for the success of the country and everyone in it. They believe that the government's job is to cover the big picture and leave the individual alone and give them a chance to succeed and prosper.

When these two philosophies are compared on their ideas and values alone, conservatism wins every time. The only way that socialist liberalism can ever win is to demonize the former group as racists, hatemongers, chauvinists, or some other scary moniker. These labels cannot possibly apply to sixty million Americans.

When a magician pulls a rabbit out of a hat, he does so by getting you to look at the flower in his lapel. That is why the Democratic Party constantly blitzes you with ridiculous stories of white supremacists and hate groups. It is the only way they can distract you from the real issues that will affect you and your children for generations.

Don't be fooled.

CONFESSION

I Have a Message for the Republican Party

I started my voting career as a Democrat but made the switch after the Bill Clinton debacle. Since then, I have pulled the lever for a straight Republican ticket. In 2016, I helped the party of my choice to win the presidency, the House and the Senate. What did they accomplish with this trifecta of political power? Very little. They have given scant support to the best president in fifty years. They have stood by and let the opposition attack him and his family unmercifully, and at this writing, are failing to provide this president critical support in the non-stop investigative efforts by the Democratic Party to destroy this administration. In fact, some of the party I helped bring to power are even disavowing support of this president in his hour of need.

I can understand how some in the party might have been reluctant when he came to power. He was an unknown quantity, and they needed to see if he was worthy of the office. But now, after accomplishing more in four years than any president in my lifetime, their reticence is inexcusable. I can only ask these spineless demagogues, what do you think would be happening if this president were a Democrat? Is there any doubt that if the Dems had elected the devil himself that they would be lining up, arm-in-arm, to defend him (or her) to the death? Of course, they would, but Republicans are not used to being in this defensive position. After all, they receive their paycheck regardless of who is in power, and I honestly think many of these '"statesmen" are weary of the daily attacks and accusations, and they long for the days when they could just show up, vote, give an occasional speech, then head to that night's ball or cocktail party.

Well, I have a message for the current leadership of the Republican Party, and it will be short and sweet. I gave you the support you needed to gain the greatest political advantage possible. Now, it is your turn. If you fail to get behind this leader of YOUR party and OUR country, and you let these partisan impeachment proceedings move forward, which CANNOT succeed without some of your party's votes, you will regret it for the next thirty years. I, for one, will abandon you FOREVER and wait for a political organization that will give me and my candidate the support that I have given them.

Don't doubt me. I am not alone.

CONFESSION

I Am Concerned about Our Country's Political Future.

My original motivation for writing this book was fairly basic. I was tired of being characterized (by association) as a racist, homophobic, deplorable, ignorant Southerner who hated almost everyone and voted for Trump because I thought he would promote this type of bigotry on a national level as I waved my rebel flag in support. This portrayal of me, my family, and my values is not only insulting, it is offensive. I felt that it was incumbent upon me to make a personal statement of my beliefs and positions on the key issues facing voters in the next election.

Along the way though, my journey took a turn or two. As a former liberal Democrat, I still felt that party was the voice of the working class, the defender of the poor, the safety net of the impoverished, and the standard bearer of the forgotten minority. But as I drilled down on the data, and examined the current economy, I couldn't help but wonder if this party wasn't just speaking to these voting blocks, but DEPENDENT on them.

At the time of this book's publication, more African Americans are employed than at any time in the history of this country, and surveys have revealed an ever-increasing popularity of Trump in this critical voting block, which was just another clue that indicated to me that prosperity in this and other minorities was not just unexpected but UNWELCOME by a party that needs voters who look to them for financial support, health insurance, and social equity.

Clearly, any political leader who provided this kind of support without a government program, a welfare check, or a guaranteed income represents the greatest threat to this party in the history of its existence. I am convinced that this is the real reason that the Democrats have spent the last four years and all of their brand equity trying to remove this president. It is obvious, by the numbers, that four more years of this kind of universal prosperity would damage that party's position irreparably, unless they choose to take a new direction that revolves around optimism, growth, and prosperity for business and the working class. It is not a new concept. Consider the words of their most charismatic leader.

But this was not my only revelation. I began to see that the party I had totally supported for almost thirty years was not exactly what I had perceived it to be. For openers, I has assumed that *"Republican"* automatically translated into *"conservative."* This is not the case. There are plenty of well-meaning, wealthy young candidates who wish to succeed in politics no matter what position they have to adopt to prevail in their district, even if it means crossing a line here and there. Further, it has become obvious to me that Republicans, as a whole, are simply not accustomed to or prepared for success if it means fighting day and night in the trenches of Congress and the Senate. Hence, I believe, is the true cause for the twenty plus retirements of incumbent Republican congressmen every election cycle.

Trump is like a new boss at a company where discipline has been lax. He snaps the whip, and suddenly, the privileged few in the front office have to show up on time, justify their positions, and report to an unforgiving boss. Trust me, I have been there, and I can tell you that most would rather see this new boss get canned than to see an increase in the firm's next quarterly report. The Republican Party is full of young (and old) statesmen who never envisioned that they would have to fight for their position daily. After all, the Republican

Party has made a science of being the minority voice for decades, even when they held the White House.

For me, the Bushes are the best example. They ran on a conservative platform and message but never challenged the status quo. The family had decades of experience in playing the Washington game of musical chairs, and they ruled without confrontation or direct political battle. They were insulted and parodied as all conservatives are, but they took it with a wry smile, which I admired at the time. Today, I look at the all-out, no-holds-barred attack the Democrats are making on a popular president, and I wonder where the Bushes' party was and why they didn't fight back. Now, I look at the Bush political dynasty and watch as THEY attack Donald Trump and wonder...has this president upset the Washington establishment so severely that even the Republican Party's iconic leaders can't tolerate his re-election? What are they afraid of?

Just as the Democrats must change to survive, so must the Republican Party, They must learn to fight tooth and nail, to rule from strength, and to support their leader even if they don't like him or her. Their opposition has learned this lesson, and if they don't, they are doomed to a second-place position, a place I fear many of them find comfortable.

All of this convinces me that this president, warts and all, is the best thing that has happened to our country and our government since Ronald Reagan. In any organization, you sometimes need to shake

things up and change the status quo, and if it had not been for Donald
Trump, I can't imagine who else would have accomplished such an
overhaul with such aplomb and efficiency.

I have read reports of Republicans who are *"tired"* of Donald Trump. I
can only wonder, what are they tired of...winning? Financial
prosperity? Full employment? A stronger military and improved trade
agreements? Maybe, they are just tired of being in office! For me, these
mealy mouthed, spineless demagogues represent the lowest form of
political animal. Let's face it...politics is an ugly business, and if you
don't support your home team in this fight, you should change parties
or retire. All this tireless rhetoric about their principles and saving the
Republic gives me gas. The average politician violates the principles of
the Constitution twice before lunch. It comes down to supporting your
president or giving the country over to the opposition. Period. If you
think Donald Trump is so bad, that it would be better to elect an
extreme left-wing socialist than to support your president, then your
constituents should send YOU home.

I have intentionally ignored the impeachment hearings underway as I
finish the final editing of this book. That is because I don't feel it
deserves any mention and is, in my opinion, the most embarrassing
political exercise I have observed in my lifetime, even surpassing the
Kavanaugh hearings, which I had thought, at the time, was the lowest
point the Congress could reach. Soon, I learned that there is no bottom
to the depths the Democratic Party will not drop to.

November 2020 will be the finish line, for the country and for the citizens who have to live with the results. I believe that the future of the nation will depend on the outcome. But the outcome will not just affect me and my fellow conservatives, but every citizen of this great country. Unless the Democrats manage to remove Trump from the ballot, I believe he will win in a huge landslide and *"down-ballot"* candidates will make this the biggest landslide in recent history. The only possible way that this doesn't happen is if the Democrats are successful in removing Trump from office, which I believe will trigger a civil war. After all, this is not Nixon. There is no crime and no president standing before a podium apologizing and resigning. This will NOT happen with Trump in office, especially with his approval numbers above fifty percent as opposed to Nixon. Trying to remove a president with the loyal allegiance that Trump enjoys will trigger a wave of protest that the country has never seen.

All of which gives me cause to worry about the strength of our democracy. Like the Roman Empire, many great democracies have eventually developed into a political maelstrom, where partisan political powers and graft eventually overtake the collective concern for the populace, at which point the prevailing parties fall into destroying each other. I can't help wondering if our great country, designed by great statesmen who had witnessed such destruction, could fall victim to the same demise by those who no longer see the greater good as superior to their political views and ambitions.

From my perspective, I wonder if a generation (or two) has not been lulled into a dream state where nothing matters but power and wealth, since most of them have never experienced global war, famine, extreme poverty, or personal loss. They could be forgiven for concluding that all that matters is political power, position, and personal ambition. It takes major loss, hunger, or national attack to bring out the true character of a statesman when the chips are down.

This is what I have to say about our country's situation today. I hope it inspires you to action.

Sincerely,
Tim Tucker

Tim Tucker is a digital marketing consultant and freelance writer who lives and works in North Carolina.